Literacy by Design™

Assessment Guide

Theme Progress Tests and Test Practice

Rigby®

A Harcourt Achieve Imprint

www.Rigby.com
1-800-531-5015

D1466003

Contents

Ongoing Test Practice

Ongoing Test Practice provides students with reading passages and questions to practice the current theme's skills. Each test includes one extended response question.

- Give the Ongoing Test Practice as homework after Lesson 7 of each theme.
- Make a transparency of the passage and questions to do more in-depth standardized test practice during class.
- Use the Answer Key on page 179 of this book to score the Ongoing Test Practice.

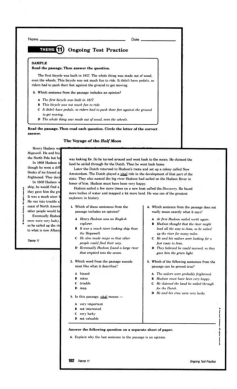

Theme Progress Tests

Theme Progress Tests cover skills and content from the student materials for each theme: comprehension, target skills, vocabulary, word study, writing, and grammar.

- Administer the Theme Progress Test on the last day of each theme.
- Two optional extended response questions may be administered with each theme.
- Extended response questions are open-book, allowing students to find text evidence to support their answers.
- Use the Student Test Record to determine students' scores using the answer key provided. Use reteaching suggestions provided for each skill if students score below the criterion score.

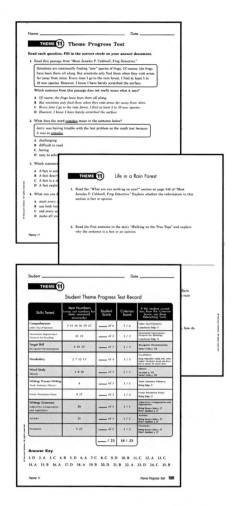

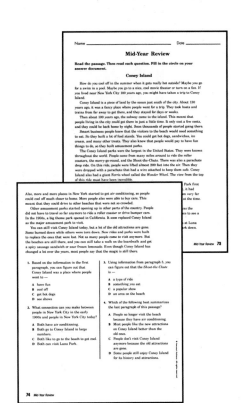

Mid-Year and End-of-Year Reviews

The Mid-Year and End-of-Year Reviews provide cumulative assessments. Students practice taking tests using new reading passages.

- The Mid-Year and End-of-Year Reviews include both extended response questions and essay prompts.
- The Student Test Record at the end of each test allows for easy scoring and provides reteaching suggestions.

Additional Resources

Test-Taking Tips and Strategies

- Pages vii and viii are blackline masters of tips and strategies students can use when taking tests.

Answer Documents

- Answer documents for Theme Progress Tests as well as Mid-Year and End-of-Year Reviews appear on pages 181 and 182 of this book.
- Copy answer documents and distribute to students at test time.
- Use a hole-punch to create a master key for each test. Place the key over each student's test to facilitate scoring.

Writing Checklist and a Lined Form for Essay Writing

- A Writing Checklist and a lined form for writing appear on pages 183 and 184 of this book.
- Distribute the Writing Checklist to students to help them write stronger essays.
- Use the lined form when administering the writing prompts found on the Mid-Year and End-of-Year Reviews.

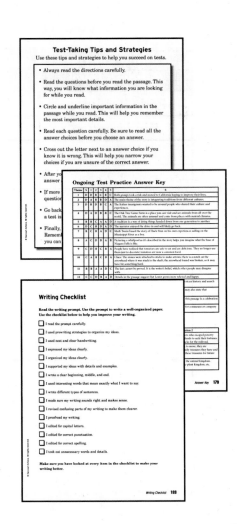

Using Rigby READS for Reading Level Placement

Ease of Student Placement

The Rigby READS (Reading Evaluation and Diagnostic System) is a valid and reliable assessment that can be administered to the whole class in a single day. On the basis of this quick and easy assessment, teachers receive the following information.

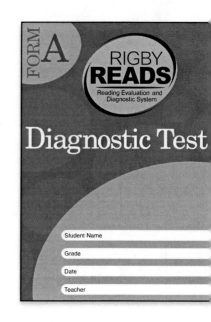

- **Placement** Each student's individual reading level for initial instruction

- **Diagnostic** A five-pillar diagnostic that pinpoints strengths and development areas in comprehension, phonics, phonemic awareness, fluency, and vocabulary

This invaluable resource is built right into the *Literacy by Design* program. Forms A and B allow you to determine end-of-year progress. The chart below shows how the Rigby READS reading levels correlate to the *Literacy by Design* reading levels.

Rigby READS Reading Level Correlation

Rigby READS Reading Level	Literacy by Design Reading Level	Rigby READS Reading Level	Literacy by Design Reading Level
Early Readiness	A	2.4	M
Kindergarten	B	3.1	N
1.1	C	3.2	O
1.2	D	3.3	P
1.3	E	4.1	Q
1.4	F	4.2	R
1.5	G	4.3	S
1.6	H	5.1	T
1.7	I	5.2	U
2.1	J	5.2	V
2.2	K	6.1	W
2.3	L		

Test-Taking Tips and Strategies

Use these tips and strategies to help you succeed on tests.

- Always read the directions carefully.

- Read the questions before you read the passage. This way, you will know what information you are looking for while you read.

- Circle and underline important information in the passage while you read. This will help you remember the most important details.

- Read each question carefully. Be sure to read all the answer choices before you choose an answer.

- Cross out the letter next to an answer choice if you know it is wrong. This will help you narrow your choices if you are unsure of the correct answer.

- After you choose an answer, reread the question and answer choice together. Do they make sense together?

- If more than one answer seems correct, read the question again. Choose the BEST answer.

- Go back and check your work if you have time. Taking a test is NOT a race to see who finishes first!

- Finally, RELAX! Taking a test can seem stressful. Remember that tests help your teacher know what you can do well and what areas you need help in.

Extended response questions ask you to write several sentences or a paragraph about a text. Use these tips to help you answer an extended response question.

- Read each question carefully.

- Use your book to review the text that the question asks about.

- Make notes before you write your answer.

- Find details and examples in the text to support your answer.

- Write your answer neatly and clearly.

- Review what you wrote. Make sure it answers the question.

- Proofread and revise your answer.

THEME ① Ongoing Test Practice

SAMPLE
Read the passage. Then answer the question.

Anna was six years old when she moved to the United States. She could only speak French. Everyone else in class spoke English. She worked hard to learn how to read and write in English. Soon she was talking and writing as if she had lived here all her life.

S. How can you connect your class to Anna's class?

A All of the students are six years old.
B None of the students speak English.
C All of the students once lived in France.
D All of the students learn about reading and writing.

Read the passage. Then read each question. Circle the letter of the correct answer.

The Gold Rush

In 1848 some people were working near the American River in California. They saw something shiny in the water. When they picked it up, they saw that it was gold. They looked around and saw that there were a lot of small pieces just sitting in the water and on the banks of the river. It was everywhere!

Soon other people heard about the gold. The news spread all over the country. By 1849 people from as far away as New York started moving out west to mine for gold. They all wanted to get rich quickly. This was the start of the gold rush.

It was not easy to go across the country back then. Trains did not go from coast to coast yet. There were no cars, planes, or paved roads back then. People had to take horses and wagons and go through dangerous places to get to the gold.

Americans were not the only people with gold fever. People from other countries also made the dangerous journey across the ocean to California. They hoped to find gold, too. They wanted to make some money and then go back home. Instead, a lot of them decided to stay in America.

Thousands of people went looking for gold. They all had to eat, sleep, and buy tools. So a lot of new hotels, restaurants, and stores opened up. This gave people places to spend the money they made from mining gold. The train companies also knew that people would pay a lot of money to take the train to California. So they built new train tracks. The state really began to <u>prosper</u>.

By the end of the gold rush, California was an important state filled with people from all over the world. People still go there today to try to make their dreams come true.

1. In what way are the people who came to California from other countries like the people who came to California from other parts of the United States?

    A Both wanted to help build train tracks across the country.
    B Both had to take a long boat trip to cross the ocean.
    C Both had to learn how to speak English.
    D Both wanted to find gold and get rich.

2. How are people who go to California today like the people who went to California in 1849?

    A They have to travel by horse and wagon.
    B They hope to make their lives better.
    C They need to buy tools when they get there.
    D They face dangers during the trip.

3. In this passage, <u>prosper</u> means —

    A find gold
    B take a long trip
    C be successful
    D build new train tracks

4. How has the trip from New York to California changed over time?

    A The trip is slower and harder now than it used to be.
    B The trip is faster and easier now than it used to be.
    C The trip is faster and harder now than it used to be.
    D The trip is slower and easier now than it used to be.

5. What is the main idea of this passage?

    A The only reason people went to California was to find gold.
    B All the people who went to California to find gold in 1849 helped make the state important.
    C People from all over the world moved to California in 1849 because they thought that they might find gold.
    D In 1849 a lot of people went looking for gold in California and got rich.

Answer the following question on a separate sheet of paper.

6. How were Americans and people from other countries similar when they came to California?

THEME **1** Theme Progress Test

Read each question. Fill in the correct circle on your answer document.

1. Which word has a short vowel sound?

   A cape

   B cap

   C dry

   D daily

2. What is the subject in the sentence below?

   > At the movie theater, Gerald and Donna pointed to a picture of a movie star.

   A movie theater

   B picture

   C Gerald and Donna

   D movie star

3. Which of the following steps should you take first when writing an essay?

   A editing

   B writing a conclusion

   C adding details

   D prewriting

4. Read this passage from "The Mystery of the Box in the Wall."

   > He handed them a dusty metal box. "It was hidden inside this wall," Papa explained, "like buried treasure."

   How is the metal box like buried treasure?

   A The metal box was hidden and held something secret.

   B The metal box contained gold coins and jewels.

   C The metal box was put in the wall by pirates.

   D The metal box was hidden underground.

5. What does the word <u>flourished</u> mean in the sentence below?

> The flowers Marta planted <u>flourished</u> because they got lots of light and she watered them every day.

A sank slowly   **C** dried quickly

B grew well   **D** smelled badly

6. Read these lines from "Samuel Goldwyn: Picture This. . ."

> Early motion pictures were quite different from today's movies. They were in black and white, not color. They had no sound, and most of them were only ten or fifteen minutes long. They didn't really tell stories, but they did show lots of action.

What connection can you make between early motion pictures and today's movies?

A Both often have music.

B Both usually tell a story.

C Both often show lots of action.

D Both usually last an hour or more.

7. Which of these lists contains words that all begin with a consonant?

A sound, form, ground   **C** ice, arrow, eggs

B action, marble, foot   **D** only, park, sound

8. When you make connections as you read, you —

A try to figure out where and when the story took place

B find words in the story you do not know and look them up in a dictionary

C relate something in the story to something you already know

D ask questions about why the author wrote the story

9. What does the word <u>ancestors</u> mean in the sentence below?

> My mother told me that one of my <u>ancestors</u> came to America with the Pilgrims on the *Mayflower*.

A hats that people used to wear on holidays

B boats that once sailed across the ocean

C children who used to live in your neighborhood

D people from your family who lived a long time ago

10. Read this passage from "Samuel Goldwyn: Picture This. . ."

> Goldwyn was hard to work with. He had strong ideas about how a movie should be made. Many other producers wanted mostly to make money, but Goldwyn wanted to make fine movies. That's just what he did. He found the best directors, he hired the most talented writers, and he used some of the biggest stars.

Which detail could you add to the passage to support the main idea?

A Goldwyn admired producers who made a lot of money from their movies.

B Goldwyn expected the best possible work from everyone involved in his movies.

C Goldwyn insisted on writing all of his movies by himself.

D Goldwyn didn't pay his actors because money wasn't important to him.

11. Which of these words has the same vowel sound as <u>trip</u>?

A trust   **C** trap

B ripe   **D** thick

12. Read these lines from the poem "Working on the Transcontinental Railroad, 1869."

> In China, I lived on the street
> Until I sailed across the sea. . . .
> In America, I swung pick and ax
> Laying miles and miles of tracks.

What connection can you make between the speaker's life in China and his life in America?

A In both places, his life was hard.

B In both places, he lost his job.

C In both places, he was rich.

D In both places, he worked for the railroad.

13. Which of these words has a short vowel sound?

A truck

B know

C cheese

D clay

14. Read these lines from "Samuel Goldwyn: Picture This. . ."

> Sam moved to Gloversville, a town in New York. Many Polish [people] found jobs in the glove factories there. Sam did too at first. Then he saw something that gave him an idea. . . .
>
> Sam wanted more than anything to live like the salesmen he saw at the Kingsborough Hotel.

What connection can you make between Sam and the other Polish people?

A Both wanted to be salesmen.

B Sam made gloves for the other Polish people.

C Both came to New York to find a better life.

D The other Polish people told Sam to move to Gloversville.

15. Which of these lists contains words that all begin with a consonant?

A idea, uncle, orange   **C** rude, smile, muddy

B glove, apple, elevator   **D** anything, grin, four

16. Which of these details should you include in an essay about where tigers live?

A A tiger's fur is orange and white with black stripes.

B Tigers can grow as big as ten feet long.

C Some tigers weigh over 500 pounds.

D Tigers are most often found in forests and swamps.

17. Read this passage from "The Mystery of the Box in the Wall."

> The Kahlos had lots of fun finding things to put in their family time capsule. They included photos of their home in Mexico, a peso, a colorful woven belt that Elena had outgrown, and other things as well.

To connect this passage to yourself, you would think about —

A what you would put in your own family time capsule

B the clothing that you have outgrown

C how many time capsules people have made

D when this story took place

18. Which word starts and ends with a consonant?

A airplane   **C** under

B pencils   **D** imagine

19. Read these passages from "Two Homes."

> "We spoke Gujarati—our Indian language—at home. We were also strict vegetarians. Still, we ate Indian food during the week and American food on the weekends."

> "I was sent to boarding school in India when I was 13. My parents felt that I needed to learn more about my Indian heritage."

What connection can you make between these two passages?

A Both passages show that the speaker's parents wanted her to stop eating American food.

B Both passages show that the speaker's parents wanted her to experience Indian culture.

C Both passages show that the speaker and her family were vegetarians.

D Both passages show that the speaker's parents missed India and wanted to move back.

Read this passage. The sentences are numbered. Answer questions 20 and 21.

> (1) Sara and Diego are best friends. (2) Their houses are next to each other. (3) Every morning they walk to school together, and then they walk home together in the afternoon. (4) They really enjoy spending time with one another.

20. Which sentence is a compound sentence?

A sentence 1

B sentence 2

C sentence 3

D sentence 4

21. What is the subject of sentence 2?

A their

B houses

C are

D each

Read these passages from "The Mystery of the Box in the Wall" and "Two Homes." Answer questions 22 and 23.

> Mr. Batali explained that everything in the box told the story of what his family's life was like a hundred years ago. Some of the old photos were pictures of the family they left in Italy when they came to America. Other photos showed what the land looked like before the house was built.

> "My parents felt that as <u>immigrants</u> they had to work hard. We all had to prove ourselves. I often felt like I had to do well for my family. I had to do well as an Indian."

22. How are the people in these passages similar?

   A They are interested in what life was like a hundred years ago.
   B Their families came to the United States from other parts of the world.
   C They felt that they had to prove themselves.
   D They kept photos of their families.

23. What does the word <u>immigrants</u> mean in the second passage?

   A people who move to a new country
   B members of a family
   C people who have children
   D men and women who work hard

Choose the word that best completes each sentence for questions 24 and 25.

24. Jafar is eight years old, and Rida is ten. Jafar and Rida can be described as _____.

   A ancestors   **C** ambitions
   B settlers   **D** youths

25. If something is shiny, you can say that it is _____.

   A flourished   **C** cautious
   B prospering   **D** gleaming

Student _____ Date _____

THEME 1

Student Theme Progress Test Record

Skills Tested	Item Numbers (cross out numbers for items answered incorrectly)	Student Score	Criterion Score	If the student scored less than the Criterion Score, use these Reteaching Tools:
Comprehension Make Connections	4 6 8 12 14 17 19 22	_____ of 8	6 / 8	**Make Connections:** Comprehension Bridge 1
Vocabulary	5 9 23 24 25	_____ of 5	4 / 5	**Vocabulary:** During independent reading time, review student's Vocabulary Journal and discuss how to improve the journal entries
Phonics Short Vowels Review	1 11 13	_____ of 3	2 / 3	**Short Vowels Review:** Sourcebook p. 15 Teacher's Guide p. 8
Initial Consonants Review	7 15 18	_____ of 3	2 / 3	**Initial Consonants Review:** Sourcebook p. 27 Teacher's Guide p. 24
Writing: Process Writing Process: Writing Process Introduction	3	_____ of 1	1 / 1	**Process: Writing Process Introduction:** Writing Bridge 1
Organizational Pattern: Main Idea and Details	10 16	_____ of 2	1 / 2	**Organizational Pattern: Main Idea and Details:** Writing Bridge 2
Writing: Grammar Simple and Compound Sentences	20	_____ of 1	1 / 1	**Simple and Compound Sentences:** Writing Resource Guide p. 1 Writer's Handbook p. 35
Simple and Compound Subjects/Predicates	2 21	_____ of 2	1 / 2	**Simple and Compound Subjects/Predicates:** Writing Resource Guide p. 2 Writer's Handbook p. 34
		_____ / 25	18 / 25	

Answer Key

1. B **2.** C **3.** D **4.** A **5.** B **6.** C **7.** A **8.** C **9.** D **10.** B **11.** D **12.** A **13.** A

14. C **15.** C **16.** D **17.** A **18.** B **19.** B **20.** C **21.** B **22.** B **23.** A **24.** D **25.** D

THEME ② Ongoing Test Practice

SAMPLE
Read the passage. Then answer the question.

The Great Wall of China is one of the biggest objects people ever made. It was built over 2,000 years ago to keep China safe. First people made it out of rocks and dirt. Then they used bricks. Today the wall is 1,500 miles long. It's big enough to see from outer space!

S. Which information is not important to the main idea of the passage?

A The Great Wall of China is one of the biggest objects ever made by people.

B It was built over 2,000 years ago to keep China safe.

C Today the wall is 1,500 miles long.

D It is so big that it can be seen from outer space.

Read the passage. Then read each question. Circle the letter of the correct answer.

Juan's Birthday Party

It was a Saturday afternoon. Juan's family was having a birthday party for him. All of his friends were there. Everyone was having a good time. Jenny stood in line for the piñata. So far no one had hit it hard enough. She could not wait for someone to break it and make the goodies fall out. Juan stood next to her. He had taken his turn and missed.

"This is cool," she said. "We never do this at my birthday parties. We just wear paper hats and eat cake."

Juan laughed.

"We eat cake, too," he said. "But it's not a real birthday party to my family unless there is a piñata. It's something that people do in Mexico. That's my mother's country of <u>origin</u>. She always had one when she was a little girl. So I get to have one every year, too. It's a lot of fun."

Jenny smiled. Then she noticed the big string of lights hanging on the fence. They were really pretty. Each light was a different color. They blinked on and off.

"What about those lights?" she asked. "Does your family put them up for birthdays, too?"

"Yes," Juan said. "They do that in the Philippines. That's where my father's family is from. The lights tell people that today is somebody's birthday in the house."

"So you mixed the ideas together," Jenny said. "Cool!"

Finally it was Jenny's turn. She put the blindfold on. Next she turned around a few times. Then she took a swing. She heard a loud thump.

Everybody started yelling. Jenny took off the blindfold. She saw the delicious treats fall to the ground. All the kids jumped in to get some. That's when Jenny decided that she would have a piñata and blinking lights at her next birthday party, too.

1. Which information in the first paragraph is not important to the story?

   A It was a Saturday afternoon.
   B Juan's family was having a birthday party for him.
   C Jenny was standing in line for the piñata.
   D Nobody had broken the piñata yet.

2. In this passage, the word <u>origin</u> means —

   A where someone is going
   B where someone is from
   C why someone is here
   D why someone did something

3. Which of these is a theme of this story?

   A putting up lights
   B learning about other cultures
   C blowing out candles
   D choosing the culture you like best

4. Which information in the last paragraph is most important to the story?

   A Everybody started yelling.
   B Jenny took off the blindfold.
   C Jenny saw the delicious treats fall to the ground.
   D Jenny decided to have a piñata and lights at her next birthday party.

5. How do you know this passage is a story?

   A It tells about characters in a setting.
   B It describes something that really happened.
   C It tells you the author's opinion.
   D It describes how to throw a birthday party.

Answer the following question on a separate sheet of paper.

6. Why is it important in the story that Juan's parents come from two countries?

THEME ② Theme Progress Test

Read each question. Fill in the correct circle on your answer document.

1. Which of these words has the same consonant blend as <u>snap</u>?

   A soon

   B snug

   C some

   D lap

2. What does the word <u>accompany</u> mean in the passage below?

   > "I am going to the library on Saturday," Fred said. "Would you like to <u>accompany</u> me?"

   A to study with

   B to play with

   C to go with

   D to talk with

3. Which of the following is a good thing to do when writing?

   A choose words that describe

   B find new ways to spell words

   C use the same words over and over again

   D write sentences that are not connected to one another

4. Read this passage from "The World on Your Plate."

   > Pasta is a very simple food to make. All you have to do is add eggs or water to flour to form a paste. (*Pasta* means "paste" in Italian.) Then you roll it out and cut it into shapes. What shapes would you choose? The strand form of spaghetti is one of the most popular shapes, but there are many others—ribbons, spirals, wheels, and tubes, to name a few. Thick or thin, straight or curly, no matter what the shape, pasta tastes great.

   Which information in this passage is most important?

   A Pasta is very simple to make.

   B *Pasta* is the Italian word for paste.

   C Pasta tastes great.

   D The strand form of spaghetti is one of the most popular shapes of pasta.

5. Which of the following would you most likely find in a story?

   A opinions and facts about an important matter
   B true information about a real person's life
   C characters and a setting
   D information about the weather

6. Which of the following best describes a theme?

   A an idea that is repeated throughout a story
   B a person who learns a lesson in a story
   C the place where a story happens
   D the problem that a person in a story has

7. Read this passage from "The World on Your Plate."

> Many of our foods, like pasta, pancakes, or bagels, are made from wheat. Another very important grain is rice. In much of the world, people eat rice every day. [People from China] helped make rice dishes popular in the United States. One of the best-known Chinese dishes is fried rice. Rice goes well with lots of food, from meats to vegetables.

What is the most important thing that the writer wants you to understand in this passage?

   A People in China enjoy eating fried rice.
   B Many of our foods are made from wheat.
   C People eat rice every day in much of the world.
   D Rice goes well with meats and vegetables.

8. Which word ends with the same sounds as <u>drop</u>?

   A draw
   B flop
   C loop
   D flip

9. To write a story, you must come up with —

   A words that rhyme
   B a good character and a bad character
   C short sentences
   D a beginning, middle, and end

10. When you write, you should always —

    A make the reader think you do not care about the people in the story
    B present your ideas in an organized way
    C try to make all of your sentences look alike
    D misspell some words

11. Which of these words has the same consonant blend as <u>poster</u>?

    A rooster   **C** posing
    B possible   **D** matter

12. Read these lines from the poem "Celebrating Our Roots: American Suitcase."

> In my suitcase
> From Ukraine, from Korea, from Spain,
> Dreams I wear every day accompany
> my fears
> my language
> my art
> my religion
> my food
> my love for this culture of many.
> *I am American.*

How are America and the countries listed in the passage connected?

    A All Americans speak the languages of the countries listed.
    B They all have the same culture.
    C American culture is made up of all of the other countries cultures.
    D They all enjoy the same food.

13. Read this passage from "The World on Your Plate."

> When Jewish people came from Europe to live in the United States, the bagel came with them. It's a circle of bread with a hole in the middle. Bagels are chewy and filling. You may like them best plain.

Which information is not important to the main idea of the passage?

    A Jewish people brought the bagel to the United States.
    B A bagel is a circle of bread with a hole in the middle.
    C A bagel is chewy and filling.
    D Some people like plain bagels best.

14. Which word contains the same consonant blend as the word <u>lost</u>?

A wander   **C** kitten

B lock   **D** blast

15. What does the word <u>necessities</u> mean in the sentence below?

> Food, water, and air are <u>necessities</u> for life.

A things you like

B things you want

C things you need

D things you have

16. What does it mean to determine importance when you read?

A find sentences in the passage that look alike

B figure out who wrote the passage

C look for words in the passage you do not know

D decide what the main ideas of the passage are

17. Which of these lists contain words that are all from the same word family?

A true, trail, trick

B looks, listens, laughs

C fun, sun, bun

D can, cat, cap

Choose the word that best completes each sentence for questions 18 and 19.

18. The line that separates two countries is called the _____.

A origin

B nationality

C border

D relocation

19. Your _____ tells people where you come from.

A belief

B border

C necessities

D nationality

Read this passage from "The World on Your Plate." Answer questions 20 and 21.

> The pizza and frankfurter came across the ocean. The tortilla crossed the border from Mexico. It's another type of pancake—but it's different from the ones you have for breakfast. Tortillas are made from corn or wheat flour. They are very thin. They're great for wraps.

20. Which detail from the passage is not important to the main idea?

   A The pizza and frankfurter came from across the ocean.
   B Tortillas are made from corn or wheat flour.
   C A tortilla is a type of pancake.
   D Tortillas are very thin.

21. What do pizza, frankfurters, and tortillas have in common?

   A Each food is a type of pancake.
   B Each food is a breakfast dish.
   C Each food came from another country.
   D Each food is great for wraps.

Read this passage. The sentences are numbered. Answer questions 22 and 23.

> (1) The barber _____ Neil's hair. (2) Neil's hair falls on the floor. (3) The barber sweeps it up with a broom. (4) The barber asks Neil how he likes his new haircut.

22. Which verb best completes sentence 1?

   A cut
   B cuts
   C cutting
   D will cut

23. What is the best way to revise sentence 3?

   A Using a broom, the barber sweeps up the hair.
   B Using a broom, he sweeps it up, the hair.
   C The barber sweeps Neil's hair.
   D The barber using a broom sweeps Neil's hair from the floor.

Read these passages from "The Fair." Answer questions 24 and 25.

> **NIKKI:** Maybe you could interview him. You could ask him questions about how mariachi bands got started, and maybe he could play little bits of songs. . . .

> **SANJAY:** That's a cool idea, Nik. My dad can play the sitar. It's kind of like an Indian guitar. He was in a band before he married my mom. His sitar has 17 strings!

24. Which of these is a theme of the two passages?

    A music from different cultures

    B interviews

    C guitars made in India

    D ideas

25. Which information is not important to the main idea of the second passage?

    A Sanjay's dad can play the sitar.

    B A sitar is like an Indian guitar.

    C Sanjay's dad was in a band before he got married.

    D His sitar has 17 strings.

Student _____ Date _____

THEME ②

Student Theme Progress Test Record

Skills Tested	Item Numbers (cross out numbers for items answered incorrectly)	Student Score	Criterion Score	If the student scored less than the Criterion Score, use these Reteaching Tools:
Comprehension Determine Importance	4 7 13 16 20 25	____ of 6	5 / 6	**Determine Importance:** Comprehension Bridge 2
Make Connections	12 21	____ of 2	1 / 2	**Make Connections:** Comprehension Bridge 1
Target Skill Identify Story Structure	9	____ of 1	1 / 1	**Identify Story Structure:** Teacher's Guide p. 49
Identify Theme	6 24	____ of 2	1 / 2	**Identify Theme:** Teacher's Guide p. 58
Vocabulary	2 15 18 19	____ of 4	3 / 4	**Vocabulary:** During independent reading time, review student's Vocabulary Journal and discuss how to improve the journal entries
Phonics Consonant Blends *sn-* and *-st*	1 11 14	____ of 3	2 / 3	**Consonant Blends** *sn-* and *-st*: Sourcebook p. 45 Teacher's Guide p. 40
Word Families	8 17	____ of 2	1 / 2	**Word Families:** Sourcebook p. 57 Teacher's Guide p. 58
Writing: Process Writing Trait: Traits Introduction	3 10	____ of 2	1 / 2	**Trait: Traits Introduction:** Writing Bridge 3
Form: Story	5	____ of 1	1 / 1	**Form: Story:** Writing Bridge 4
Writing: Grammar Subject-Verb Agreement	22	____ of 1	1 / 1	**Subject-Verb Agreement:** Writing Resource Guide p. 3 Writer's Handbook p. 24
Review Sentence Structure	23	____ of 1	1 / 1	**Sentence Structure:** Writing Resource Guide p. 4 Writer's Handbook p. 46
		____ / 25	18 / 25	

Answer Key

1. B   2. C   3. A   4. A   5. C   6. A   7. C   8. B   9. D   10. B   11. A   12. C   13. D

14. D   15. C   16. D   17. C   18. C   19. D   20. A   21. C   22. B   23. A   24. A   25. C

THEME ③ Ongoing Test Practice

SAMPLE
Read the passage. Then answer the question.

Tina got out of bed and rushed to the window. When she looked outside, she saw that everything was covered in a blanket of white. She could see her father shoveling the sidewalk as cars drove slowly by. Tina knew that there would be no school today.

S. Based on the information in the passage, you can figure out that —

  A Tina is sad that school is cancelled
  B Tina's father put a white blanket on the sidewalk
  C the streets are covered with mud
  D there was a snowstorm last night

Read the passage. Then read each question. Circle the letter of the correct answer.

Little Italy

Have you ever heard of a place called Little Italy? It is not a country. It is not even a village or a town. It is a part of a city in the United States where people cook, act, and talk a lot like they do in Italy. There are many cities all over the country that have an area called Little Italy.

People came up with the name about 100 years ago when many Italians started moving to the United States. Most of these Italian immigrants went to live in big cities. Many of them found homes near one another. In some places everybody on the block came from the same part of Italy. They opened up their own stores and places to eat. They played their music together, and they went to church together. They formed their own neighborhoods, so it was almost like they were still back home. This is how neighborhoods became known as Little Italy.

The children of these Italian immigrants grew up and learned about life in the United States. They also learned about the country that their parents came from. They kept up the way of life that their family had taught them. Soon a lot of other people came to the neighborhood. They wanted to enjoy everything it had to offer. They shopped in the stores. They ate the food. They danced to the music and admired the art. Today many cities across the country have a part of town called Little Italy. They are easy to <u>identify</u> because there are signs and flags everywhere.

There are also other neighborhoods in big cities in the United States that are or once were mostly made up of people from a different country. For example, you can visit Chinatown in many major American cities and see things that you might only see in China. You can get Chinese food and clothes, and you will also probably hear a lot of people speaking Chinese.

So the next time you are in a big city, look around at the neighborhoods. It's almost like taking a short tour of the world!

1. Italian immigrants probably came to the United States to —

   A visit Little Italy and Chinatown
   B make a better life for themselves
   C show Americans what life is like in Italy
   D see what it was like to live in a big city

2. What can you infer about immigrants who lived in Little Italy?

   A They wanted to leave the United States and move to another part of the world.
   B They wanted to blend in with other people who lived in the city.
   C They liked to live quietly, without a lot of music and parties.
   D They wanted their lives in the United States to be a lot like they were in Italy.

3. In this passage, <u>identify</u> means —

   A lose
   B recognize
   C buy
   D explain

4. What can you infer about the kinds of restaurants you would find in a city's Chinatown?

   A They sell mostly foods like pizza and spaghetti.
   B They sell food only to people who live in Chinatown.
   C Many of them serve Chinese food.
   D The people who work at the restaurants live in Little Italy.

5. Why do so many people probably like visiting Little Italy?

   A They enjoy experiencing the culture.
   B It's less expensive than traveling to Italy.
   C They want to learn to speak Italian.
   D They enjoy shopping.

Answer the following question on a separate sheet of paper.

6. Why did Italians probably settle in the same city neighborhoods?

THEME ③ Theme Progress Test

Read each question. Fill in the correct circle on your answer document.

1. What does the word <u>abandon</u> mean in the sentence below?

> The sun was so hot that day that we decided to <u>abandon</u> our shoes and run barefoot in the grass.

  A forget to bring

  B carry away

  C leave behind

  D put on

2. Which of the following are you most likely to find in a report?

  A a discussion of many different topics

  B characters that are make-believe

  C facts and information about a topic

  D sentences that end in rhyming words

3. Read this sentence.

> When I went to the store, I bought some red laces for my shoes.

Which of the following words from the sentence has a long vowel sound?

  A laces

  B red

  C went

  D some

4. What does a noun do?

  A It describes the way that something is being done.

  B It tells about an action.

  C It describes what something looks or feels like.

  D It names a person, place, thing, or idea.

5. What does it mean to make an inference when you read?

    A decide whether information in a sentence is important or just interesting

    B figure something out based on what you read and what you already know

    C identify the beginning, middle, and end of the story you have read

    D make a connection between two texts that you have read

6. Which of these words has a long vowel sound?

    A chin

    B fast

    C ten

    D race

7. Read this passage from "Weird Animals."

> The grasshopper mouse lives in North America. Unlike an ordinary mouse, it is a mighty hunter with sharp teeth and big jaw muscles! Grasshopper mice like to eat grasshoppers, insects, lizards, and scorpions. It does not squeak. It stands up on its back legs and HOWLS! Its roar can be heard more than 100 yards away!

The grasshopper mouse probably got its name from —

    A what it sounds like

    B where it lives

    C what it likes to eat

    D what it looks like

8. When you write a report, you should —

    A tell a story

    B give the reader facts

    C explain your opinion

    D write about many different topics

9. Which of these lists contains words that are all nouns?

    A glass, chair, kitten

    B sleep, strong, whisper

    C blue, write, run

    D angry, funny, noisy

10. Read these lines from the poem "Vertebrate, or Invertebrate—What's My ID?"

> I hatch from a cocoon but do not fly.
> I love still waters and hate the dry.
> I have sharp teeth in my grin.
> I use those teeth to bite through skin. . . .
> My body's divided into thirty-four parts.
> Drs. still use me to heal what hurts.

You can infer that the speaker in this poem —

A lives somewhere very cold

B is a mosquito

C lives in the desert

D lives in a pond

11. Which words in the sentence below are nouns?

> After a hard day at school, Kara just wanted to go home and nap.

A hard, school, wanted, nap

B after, school, Kara, nap

C day, school, Kara, home

D day, school, wanted, home

12. What does the word <u>variety</u> mean in the sentence below?

> Basil had a <u>variety</u> of chores to do, including cleaning his room, painting the garage, and watering the plants.

A group of difficult things

B group of different things

C group of fun things

D group of dangerous things

13. Read the sentence.

> Kiri said that he plans to write an essay about bears.

Which of these words from the sentence has a long vowel sound?

A said

B that

C plans

D write

Read the passage. The sentences are numbered. Answer questions 14 and 15.

> (1) Have you ever been to the Grand Canyon. (2) It is really an amazing place! (3) It is more than 5,000 feet deep. (4) You should really visit it someday?

14. What is the best way to rewrite sentence 1?

    A Have you ever been to the Grand Canyon?

    B Have you ever been to the grand canyon.

    C Have ever been to the Grand Canyon.

    D Has you ever been to the Grand Canyon.

15. What is the best way to rewrite sentence 4?

    A Someday you should really visit it?

    B Should you really visit it someday!

    C Should you really visit it someday.

    D You should really visit it someday.

Read this passage from "Slimy, Spiny Riddles." Answer questions 16 and 17.

> "A leech!" Uncle Isaac plucked out a fat, slick, wormlike creature. "Isn't it a beauty?". . .
>
> "Humans have used leeches in medicine for centuries. Today doctors mainly use them after some tricky operations. The leech sucks the extra blood from the wound to reduce swelling." Uncle Isaac put the leech back into the aquarium.

16. Based on the information in this passage, you can infer that —

    A Uncle Isaac is afraid of leeches

    B too much blood in a wound causes swelling

    C leeches are very large and can fly

    D a leech is a type of medicine

17. Which information is most important in this passage?

    A Doctors sometimes use leeches in medicine.

    B Leeches are fat and slick.

    C Uncle Isaac keeps the leech in an aquarium.

    D Doctors sometimes perform tricky operations.

Read this passage from "Animals." Answer questions 18 and 19.

> Scientists divide the living world into groups. Each group shares certain traits. Such groupings make it easier to study and compare living things. The largest kind of group is called a kingdom. All animals are considered part of the animal kingdom.

18. Using the information in this passage, you can figure out that —

   A there are many different types of animal kingdoms
   B there are five plant kingdoms
   C all living things are part of the animal kingdom
   D birds are part of the animal kingdom

19. Which of the following details could you add to the passage to support the main idea?

   A Scientists study ocean life.
   B Only large animals are part of the animal kingdom.
   C There are five kingdoms of living things.
   D Animals need food and water to survive.

Choose the word that best completes each sentence for questions 20 and 21.

20. When you put things in groups, you _____ them.

   A abandon
   B categorize
   C identify
   D species

21. A group of animals that shares similar traits or qualities is called a _____.

   A researcher
   B species
   C characteristics
   D variety

Read this passage from "Animals." Answer questions 22 and 23.

Many other <u>invertebrates</u> have skeletons that cover the outside of their bodies like plates of armor. Crabs, spiders, and bees all have outside skeletons. Scientists group these animals together because they have legs with joints that help them to walk, swim, or jump. Scientists then divide them into subgroups based on how many legs they have.

22. What can you infer about crabs, spiders, and bees?

   A They all have hard shells.
   B They all have large eyes.
   C They are all good swimmers.
   D They all have the same number of legs.

23. <u>Invertebrates</u> are animals that —

   A can swim
   B can jump
   C have no backbone
   D have skeletons

Read this passage from "Slimy, Spiny Riddles." Answer questions 24 and 25.

Suddenly, Pete noticed a brown insect clinging to a branch. "A walking stick! I couldn't see it because it's camouflaged."

"Right you are, Pete," Uncle Isaac said. "Walking sticks are one of the longest insects. When they hatch from their eggs, they hide in leaves, so they're usually green. Only later do they turn brown."

24. What is the most important information in this passage?

   A Pete noticed a brown insect.
   B Walking sticks blend in with their surroundings.
   C Walking sticks hatch from eggs and then hide in leaves.
   D Walking sticks start out green and then turn brown.

25. What can you infer about walking sticks?

   A Their appearance helps protect them from other animals.
   B Their diet is made up mostly of meat and vegetables.
   C They live in dry, sandy places without plants.
   D They are one of the smallest insects in the world.

Student _____ Date _____

Student Theme Progress Test Record

Skills Tested	Item Numbers (cross out numbers for items answered incorrectly)	Student Score	Criterion Score	If the student scored less than the Criterion Score, use these Reteaching Tools:
Comprehension Infer	5 7 10 16 18 22 25	___ of 7	5 / 7	**Infer:** Comprehension Bridge 3
Determine Importance	17 24	___ of 2	1 / 2	**Determine Importance:** Comprehension Bridge 2
Vocabulary	1 12 20 21 23	___ of 5	4 / 5	**Vocabulary:** During independent reading time, review student's Vocabulary Journal and discuss how to improve the journal entries
Phonics Long Vowels	3 6 13	___ of 3	2 / 3	**Long Vowels:** Sourcebook p. 77 Teacher's Guide p. 74
Writing: Process Writing Trait: Ideas	19	___ of 1	1 / 1	**Trait: Ideas:** Writing Bridge 5
Form: Report	2 8	___ of 2	1 / 2	**Form: Report:** Writing Bridge 6
Writing: Grammar Declarative/Interrogative Sentences	14	___ of 1	1 / 1	**Declarative/Interrogative Sentences:** Writing Resource Guide p. 5 Writer's Handbook p. 35
Imperative/Exclamatory Sentences	15	___ of 1	1 / 1	**Imperative/Exclamatory Sentences:** Writing Resource Guide p. 6 Writer's Handbook p. 36
Nouns	4 9 11	___ of 3	2 / 3	**Nouns:** Writing Resource Guide p. 12 Writer's Handbook p. 20
		___ / 25	18 / 25	

Answer Key

1. C   2. C   3. A   4. D   5. B   6. D   7. C   8. B   9. A   10. D   11. C   12. B   13. D

14. A   15. D   16. B   17. A   18. D   19. C   20. B   21. B   22. A   23. C   24. B   25. A

THEME ④ Ongoing Test Practice

SAMPLE
Read the passage. Then answer the question.

Paul was trying to fall asleep, but he was not having much luck. Outside, the wind whistled low and the branches of the tree groaned. Dry leaves scraped the street as they blew slowly down the block. "It's going to be a long night," he thought.

S. The writer of this passage wants you to imagine —

    A what Paul sees

    B what Paul smells

    C what Paul tastes

    D what Paul hears

Read the passage. Then read each question. Circle the letter of the correct answer.

The Oak Tree Game Farm

Jose and Linda sat on the bus beside their mother. The hard seats shook softly with every turn. It was a warm summer day, and they were going to the Oak Park Game Farm.

"I haven't been there in a long time," Jose said to his younger sister. "But it's a lot of fun."

"What is a game farm, anyway?" Linda asked their mother.

"It's a place where they have animals for you to see," their mother answered. "Most of them are the kinds of animals that you'd see in a forest or a meadow. They have to be able to live in the <u>conditions</u> in this part of the country. Animals that come from places that are always very cold or very hot wouldn't be happy living around here."

"The farm also has animals from other parts of the world," Jose added. "Some of them are really interesting. I've been reading all about them. One of them is called the kudu. It's a kind of antelope."

"An antelope? What's that?" Linda asked. It was a word that she had never heard before. She was sure her brother could explain it to her. He knew about a lot of things because he read so many books. Jose was a walking, talking encyclopedia.

"It's kind of like a cross between a goat and a deer," he said. "It has short hair and long horns. There are spots and stripes on its fur and there is a white patch on its face."

"What other kinds of animals do they have at the game farm?" Linda wondered.

"There are some small, brightly colored birds that I think you will like," Jose said. "They are called rainbow lorikeets, and they make a kind of chattering sound when they are just hanging out. When the lorikeets eat, they make a loud screeching noise. But don't worry, they're friendly."

As Jose finished speaking, the bus slowed and then turned into a large parking lot. They were there! The family got off the bus and headed to the gate. Jose, Linda, and their mother were going to have a wonderful day at the game farm.

1. In the first paragraph, why does the writer describe the seats on the bus?

   A So you understand how riding on the bus feels.
   B So you know the bus is making many turns.
   C So you can figure out where the bus is going.
   D So you know who is sitting in the seats.

2. Which of these sentences from the passage includes a metaphor?

   A *"What is a game farm, anyway?" Linda asked.*
   B *I've been reading all about them.*
   C *It has short hair and long horns.*
   D *He was a walking, talking encyclopedia.*

3. How does Linda feel when she asks Jose what an antelope is?

   A sad   C angry
   B curious   D scared

4. What does the word conditions mean in this passage?

   A animals in the forest
   B things that affect the way you live
   C the places where you have been
   D things that make you happy

5. Why does Jose describe the kudu as a cross between a goat and a deer?

   A So you can imagine what the kudu smells like.
   B So you can imagine what the kudu sounds like.
   C So you can imagine what the kudu looks like.
   D So you can imagine what the kudu feels like.

Answer the following question on a separate sheet of paper.

6. If you were to tell a friend about the Oak Tree Game Farm, how would you describe it?

THEME **4** Theme Progress Test

Read each question. Fill in the correct circle on your answer document.

1. Creating images in your mind as you read helps you —

   A find examples of dialogue in a text
   B understand and remember what you read
   C identify the main character in a text
   D locate words that are spelled incorrectly in what you read

2. What does the word <u>century</u> mean in the sentence below?

   > It was the biggest storm that had hit the city in over a <u>century</u>.

   A 24 hours
   B 7 days
   C 12 months
   D 100 years

3. Which words in the sentence below are proper nouns?

   > The Johnson family invited us to come to their house for Thanksgiving dinner on Thursday afternoon.

   A The, Johnson, Thanksgiving
   B family, house, dinner
   C Johnson, Thanksgiving, Thursday
   D invited, come, dinner

4. Which words would you most likely see in a passage where events are arranged by sequence?

   A first, then, finally
   B once, again, some
   C I, me, mine
   D to, from, for

5. Which type of reference book should you use to find the meaning of a word you do not know?

   A encyclopedia
   B almanac
   C dictionary
   D thesaurus

6. An author is going to write about giant redwood trees. What is a prewriting step the author might use?

   A The author will look for misspelled words.
   B The author will write his or her conclusion.
   C The author will delete sentences that aren't important to his or her main point.
   D The author will write down ideas about giant redwood trees.

7. What does the word <u>adapt</u> mean in the sentence below?

   > When a cat moves into a new house, it can take it a few days to <u>adapt</u> to its new surroundings.

   A find
   B ignore
   C adjust
   D frighten

8. What does it mean when you organize your writing by sequence?

   A You put events in order from most important to least important.
   B You put events in a mixed-up order.
   C You put events in order from least important to most important.
   D You put events in the order that they happen.

9. Read this passage from "The Pea Blossom."

   > "Whee, I'm flying!" shouted the pea. "Catch me if you can!"

   What can you tell about the pea from the way the pea speaks in this passage?

   A The pea is having fun.
   B The pea is scared.
   C The pea is curious.
   D The pea is angry.

10. Read this passage from "Mrs. McClary's Very Weird Garden."

> "So the plants develop ways to trap insects for food. Take my sundew.
> It traps insects with little sticky hairs on its leaves. . . ."
>
> Just then a fly landed on a scary-looking sundew. Its legs became trapped in goo.

Which words from the passage help you imagine what a sundew feels like?

A *insect, food, fly*

B *sticky hairs, trapped in goo*

C *develop ways, trap, leaves*

D *plant, scary-looking*

11. Which words in the sentences below are proper nouns?

> Last September, Aaron and his family moved. They loaded their furniture
> into a big truck and drove it to their new home in Atlanta.

A September, Aaron, Atlanta

B moved, loaded, drove

C family, furniture, truck

D his, their, it

12. If you wanted to find out what eagles eat, you would look in —

A a dictionary

B an almanac

C an encyclopedia

D an atlas

13. Which words in the passage below are proper nouns?

> As Sarah walked to the park on Saturday morning, she was happy the
> weather was nice and sunny. She was meeting her sister Ellen to fly a kite
> in front of their favorite statue.

A She, her, their

B Sarah, Saturday, Ellen

C park, weather, statue

D happy, nice, sunny

Read this passage from "The Pea Blossom." Answer questions 14 and 15.

> The old man agreed as he looked from the plant to his daughter, and again to the plant. Could it be that as the plant grew colorful, the color returned to his daughter's cheeks? He could not be certain; perhaps his hopes were fooling his eyes.

14. What does the writer want you to picture as you read this passage?

   A the sound the old man made when he looked at the plant and his daughter
   B the smell that filled the room as the plant grew larger over time
   C what the old man saw as he looked at the plant and his daughter
   D where the old man was sitting when he looked at the plant and his daughter

15. Based on the information in this passage, you can infer that —

   A the daughter had been sick
   B the plant used to be bigger
   C the old man is concerned about the plant
   D the old man works as a gardener

Read this passage from "Ode to the Giant Redwood." Answer questions 16 and 17.

> An army of giants as far as I can see.
> Silent, proud soldier never able to break free.
> With strong, thick arms stretched so high,
> You brush your rough hands against the sky.
> For centuries you've towered evergreen.
> If you could speak! What battles you've seen!

16. Which words in this passage help you imagine what the trees look like?

   A *proud, brush, speak*
   B *centuries, evergreen, seen*
   C *never, strong, against*
   D *giants, towered, evergreen*

17. Why does the author compare the tree to a soldier?

   A because the tree is in a forest near an army base
   B because the tree looks like it is wearing a uniform
   C because the tree is strong and sturdy like a soldier
   D because the tree was planted after a war ended

Read this passage from "Waking Up a Bean." Answer questions 18 and 19.

> The store had lots of different kinds of dried beans. I chose red kidney beans. I like their shape and their reddish-brown color. Kidney beans are also good for experiments. The beans grow fairly quickly. I'm really excited about this experiment. I'm a little nervous, too. I have never done an experiment on my own before.

18. Based on the information in this passage, you can figure out that the speaker is —

   A a scientist
   B a student
   C a grocery store clerk
   D a farmer

19. What words in the passage help you create an image of the kidney beans?

   A *excited, nervous, before*
   B *fairly, quickly, really*
   C *different, grow, experiments*
   D *dried, shape, reddish-brown*

Read this passage from "The Pea Blossom." Answer questions 20 and 21.

> Then one day, "CRACK!" The pod suddenly burst open and the five peas tumbled into a young boy's hand.
>
> "Excellent!" the boy exclaimed, "these peas are perfect for my new pea shooter." He slipped a pea into the shooter, puffed into it, and sent the pea in a high arch across the garden.

20. Why does the writer use the words *crack* and *burst* in this passage?

   A She wants you to imagine that the peas were not able to get out of the pod.
   B She wants you to wonder why the boy used the peas in his pea shooter.
   C She wants you to understand how fast and hard the pod opened.
   D She wants you to picture what the pea looked like as it flew through the air.

21. What can you tell about the boy from the way he speaks in this passage?

   A The boy is excited.
   B The boy is concerned.
   C The boy is frightened.
   D The boy is weary.

Read this passage. The sentences are numbered. Answer questions 22 and 23.

(1) Jen made sure to wake up early this morning. (2) Jen has a lot of things to do today. (3) She has to return her library books and get some groceries. (4) She also has to take her dog to the vet to get a shot.

22. What is the best way to combine sentences 1 and 2?

  A Jen made sure to wake up early this morning, but she has a lot of things to do today.

  B Jen made sure to wake up early this morning because she has a lot of things to do today.

  C Jen made sure to wake up and she woke up early because she has a lot of things to do today.

  D Jen made sure to wake up early this morning, and Jen has a lot of things to do today.

23. What is the best way to combine sentences 3 and 4?

  A She has to return her library books and get some groceries and take her dog to the vet to get a shot.

  B She has to return her library books get some groceries take her dog to the vet to get a shot.

  C She has to return her library books and get some groceries in order to take her dog to the vet to get a shot.

  D She has to return her library books, get some groceries, and take her dog to the vet to get a shot.

Choose the word that best completes each sentence for questions 24 and 25.

24. Maria planted the flower seeds outside because she knew they needed plenty of sunlight and water in order to _____.

  A pollinate
  B germinate
  C adapt
  D require

25. The seeds of the pine tree are found in its _____.

  A cones
  B criteria
  C conditions
  D equipment

Student _____ Date _____

THEME **4**

Student Theme Progress Test Record

Skills Tested	Item Numbers (cross out numbers for items answered incorrectly)	Student Score	Criterion Score	If the student scored less than the Criterion Score, use these Reteaching Tools:
Comprehension Create Images	1 10 14 16 19 20	_____ of 6	5 / 6	**Create Images:** Comprehension Bridge 4
Infer	15 18	_____ of 2	2 / 2	**Infer:** Comprehension Bridge 3
Target Skill Understand Use of Dialogue	9 21	_____ of 2	1 / 2	**Understand Use of Dialogue:** Teacher's Guide p. 115
Understand Metaphor	17	_____ of 1	1 / 1	**Understand Metaphor:** Teacher's Guide p. 124
Vocabulary	2 7 24 25	_____ of 4	3 / 4	**Vocabulary:** During independent reading time, review student's Vocabulary Journal and discuss how to improve the journal entries
Word Study Reference Materials	5 12	_____ of 2	1 / 2	**Reference Materials:** Sourcebook p. 119 Teacher's Guide p. 122
Writing: Process Writing Process: Prewriting	6	_____ of 1	1 / 1	**Process: Prewriting:** Writing Bridge 7
Organizational Pattern: Sequence	4 8	_____ of 2	1 / 2	**Organizational Pattern: Sequence:** Writing Bridge 8
Writing: Grammar Sentence Combining	22 23	_____ of 2	1 / 2	**Sentence Combining:** Writing Resource Guide p. 7 Writer's Handbook p. 45
Proper Nouns	3 11 13	_____ of 3	2 / 3	**Proper Nouns:** Writing Resource Guide p. 9 Writer's Handbook p. 4
		_____ / 25	18 / 25	

Answer Key

1. B   2. D   3. C   4. A   5. C   6. D   7. C   8. D   9. A   10. B   11. A   12. C   13. B

14. C   15. A   16. D   17. C   18. B   19. D   20. C   21. A   22. B   23. D   24. B   25. A

THEME ⑤ Ongoing Test Practice

SAMPLE
Read the passage. Then answer the question.

In 1862 America passed a new law. It was called the Homestead Act. This law said that people could go out west and build houses. If they lived there for at least five years, they would own the land. This law helped people spread out all over the country.

S. Based on the information in the passage, you can figure out that a homestead is a —

A law   **C** country

B house   **D** town

Read the passage. Then read each question. Circle the letter of the correct answer.

Jelly, Jam, or Marmalade?

One of the most popular lunch foods is the sandwich. For kids, peanut butter is a favorite sandwich ingredient. But when you have a peanut butter sandwich, what else do you put on it? Jelly, jam, and marmalade have long been favorite sandwich toppings, but each is a little different from the other.

So what is the difference between jelly and jam? First of all, they look different. Jelly is <u>smooth</u>, and jam is not. Jam has pieces of fruit in it. When you look closely at jam, you can see seeds in it. The seeds come from the fruit that the jam was made from. That is the second difference between jelly and jam. Even though they are both made from fruit, they are cooked in different ways and have different <u>ingredients</u>. When you make jam, you crush the fruit. Then you boil the pieces. When you make jelly, you drain the juice from the fruit. Then you heat the juice. Next you add syrup. When the mixture cools, it turns into jelly.

But maybe you would rather have marmalade with your peanut butter. Marmalade is usually made from oranges. To make it, you cut up an orange but do not peel the <u>rind</u> off. Next you crush the pieces of fruit into very tiny pieces. Nobody wants a big chunk of orange peel in their sandwich! Then you boil the small pieces of fruit. In the end, you have a sticky substance that tastes great when you spread it on bread.

One thing jelly, jam, and marmalade all have in common is that they were first made for the same reason. Hundreds of years ago, people had no way to keep fruit cold and fresh without freezing it. They had to think of things to mix into fruit so that it would stay fresh during the winter. Even though we have refrigerators now to keep fruit cold, the ways of making jam, jelly, and marmalade are <u>traditions</u> people follow today. We teach people to make the spreads the same way people did in the past because they taste so good.

1. Read this sentence.

> Jelly, jam, and marmalade have long been favorite sandwich toppings, but each is a little <u>different</u> from the other.

Which of these words is an antonym of <u>different</u>?

A unlike

B same

C dislike

D many

2. Based on the passage, you can figure out that marmalade is a type of —

A bread

B peanut butter

C fruit spread

D orange

3. Based on the information in the passage, you can figure out that <u>rind</u> means —

A fruit peel

B leaf

C fruit syrup

D orange

4. Read the meanings below for the word <u>smooth</u>.

> **smooth**
>
> 1. without lumps 2. without problems 3. steady 4. without hair

Which meaning best fits the way <u>smooth</u> is used in the passage?

A meaning 1

B meaning 2

C meaning 3

D meaning 4

5. Using clues from the passage, you can figure out that <u>ingredients</u> are —

A kinds of juice

B kinds of jelly

C seeds from fruit

D parts of a mix

Answer the following question on a separate sheet of paper.

6. Use clues from the passage to explain what a <u>tradition</u> is.

THEME ⑤ Theme Progress Test

Read each question. Fill in the correct circle on your answer document.

1. Which of these words is a synonym for <u>friendly</u>?

   A quiet

   B mean

   C pleasant

   D funny

2. Which word in the sentence is a proper noun?

   > The students worked together to write a play about Abraham Lincoln.

   A students

   B Abraham Lincoln

   C play

   D together

3. When you write, what is the purpose of drafting?

   A to fill in missing details

   B to help you find misspelled words

   C to practice writing neatly

   D to help you figure out what you want to say

4. Read this passage from "The Superstition Mountains."

   > She told us that the mountains are a group of peaks, cliffs, and mesas. There isn't a single <u>summit</u>, even though people sometimes talk about Superstition Mountain. The mountains are located on the edge of a vast wilderness area. She said there is also a great state park at the base of the mountains.

   Which words from the passage help you figure out the meaning of <u>summit</u>?

   A *peaks, mountains*

   B *park, wilderness*

   C *group, vast*

   D *edge, base*

5. Which of these examples is most like a personal narrative?

    A a report about animals that live in the zoo

    B a story about a trip you took to the park

    C an article about the best soccer player at your school

    D an essay about a famous scientist

6. What does it mean to use fix-up strategies when you read?

    A to summarize the important parts of a text

    B to explain the author's purpose for writing

    C to correct errors you find in a text

    D to use clues in a text to help you figure out difficult words

7. What does the word <u>light</u> mean in the sentence below?

> Even though the box was very big, I could carry it because it was <u>light</u>.

    A a lamp

    B not heavy

    C beams from the sun

    D not dark

8. Read this sentence.

> The <u>quick</u> runner won the race.

Which of the following words is a synonym for <u>quick</u>?

    A slow

    B swift

    C sprint

    D champion

9. A large, level area of high land is called a —

    A plateau

    B region

    C canyon

    D climate

10. When you write a personal narrative, you —

  A describe an event you read about in the news.
  B write about a character you made up
  C explain to the reader how something works
  D tell the story of a true event you took part in

11. What does the word <u>trip</u> mean in the sentence below?

  > Hector and his family took a <u>trip</u> to the desert last fall.

  A a train
  B a mistake
  C to stumble
  D a vacation

12. Read these lines from the song "This Land Is Your Land."

  > As I go walking this ribbon of highway
  > I see above me this endless skyway
  > And all around me the wind keeps saying:
  > "This land is made for you and me."

  The author of this song wants you to imagine someone —

  A traveling in a wide open land
  B flying through the sky
  C driving on a busy road
  D wrapping a present

13. Read this passage from "Take a Virtual Trip."

  > These mountains are younger and taller than the Appalachian Mountains.
  > The climate in the area is drier, too. Not as much rain has eroded the
  > rugged peaks.

  Based on clues in the passage, you can figure out that when mountains
  erode, they —

  A get wet
  B wear away
  C dry out
  D grow larger

14. Read this passage from "Who Believes in Buried Treasure?"

> I groaned and climbed over another rock. I am a city girl who likes malls and museums. So why was I dressed like a coal miner and following my cousin Mateo and my grandmother up a mountain?

How does the author show that the girl is not happy to be climbing the mountain?

A by calling her a coal miner
B by telling you that she is upset
C by describing the sound she makes
D by telling you that she likes malls and museums

15. Which of these words is an antonym of <u>quiet</u>?

A silent
B shy
C loud
D peaceful

16. What does the word <u>impact</u> mean in the sentence below?

> The storm had an <u>impact</u> on our fishing trip, and we had to go home early.

A an effect
B heavy rainfall
C a scary event
D a crash

17. Read this passage from "Who Believes in Buried Treasure?"

> He took off with me so close behind him that when he stopped suddenly, I crashed into him. The [crash] sent us falling over the edge. Suddenly we were sliding and tumbling down a chute like one at our waterpark—but without the water.

Based on clues in the passage, you can figure out that *chute* means —

A cliff
B slip
C slide
D ladder

Read this passage from "Take a Virtual Trip." Answer questions 18 and 19.

> Holding your breath, you stay <u>close</u> to the rock wall. You pass limestone, sandstone, and <u>shale</u>. The minerals in each kind of rock color the cliff wall in shades of red, yellow, and green. As you go lower and lower into the canyon, you know you are passing through history. The rocks near the top formed several hundred million years ago.

18. Which meaning does the word <u>close</u> have in this passage?

  A near

  B shut

  C alike

  D almost

19. Which words from the passage best help you understand what <u>shale</u> is?

  A *red, yellow, green*

  B *limestone, sandstone, kind of rock*

  C *holding your breath, stay, pass*

  D *history, formed, years ago*

Read this passage. The sentences are numbered. Answer questions 20 and 21.

> (1) We were camping at Blackstone Park one night when my sisters Kara and Sara said they saw a bear. (2) They said it was behind the tent. (3) When I went to look, I saw that the girls had put Kara's teddy bear on a tree stump. (4) We all had a good laugh at their joke.

20. Which of these words from sentence 1 is a common noun?

  A Blackstone

  B night

  C Kara

  D saw

21. Which word in sentence 3 is a plural noun?

  A girls

  B bear

  C tree

  D stump

Read this passage from "Take a Virtual Trip." Answer questions 22 and 23.

> The next stop on your <u>trip</u> takes you to a cavern. . . . Shivering, you go down a rocky stairway. White <u>stalactites</u> hang from the ceiling. The layers of limestone around you formed millions of years ago.

22. The author of this passage uses descriptive words to make you —

   A think you are underwater
   B worry about the safety of a character
   C feel like you are walking in a cave
   D wonder how a cave is made

23. By reading on in this passage, you can figure out that <u>stalactites</u> are —

   A a kind of stairway made of rock
   B a kind of ice found in caves
   C a kind of light that attaches to a ceiling
   D a kind of rock that hangs down in a cave

Choose the word that best completes each sentence for questions 24 and 25.

24. A very large valley is called a _____.

   A solution
   C plateau
   B region
   D canyon

25. The typical pattern of weather in a place is known as its _____.

   A aspect
   C climate
   B plateau
   D region

Student _____   Date _____

Student Theme Progress Test Record

Skills Tested	Item Numbers (cross out numbers for items answered incorrectly)	Student Score	Criterion Score	If the student scored less than the Criterion Score, use these Reteaching Tools:
Comprehension Use Fix-Up Strategies	4 6 13 17 19 23	___ of 6	5 / 6	**Use Fix-Up Strategies:** Comprehension Bridge 5
Create Images	12 14 22	___ of 3	2 / 3	**Create Images:** Comprehension Bridge 4
Vocabulary	9 16 24 25	___ of 4	3 / 4	**Vocabulary:** During independent reading time, review student's Vocabulary Journal and discuss how to improve the journal entries
Word Study Synonyms and Antonyms	1 8 15	___ of 3	2 / 3	**Synonyms and Antonyms:** Sourcebook p. 139 Teacher's Guide p. 140
Multiple-Meaning Words	7 11 18	___ of 3	2 / 3	**Multiple-Meaning Words:** Sourcebook p. 151 Teacher's Guide p. 156
Writing: Process Writing Process: Drafting	3	___ of 1	1 / 1	**Process: Drafting:** Writing Bridge 9
Form: Personal Narrative	5 10	___ of 2	1 / 2	**Form: Personal Narrative:** Writing Bridge 10
Writing: Grammar Common and Proper Nouns	2 20	___ of 2	1 / 2	**Common and Proper Nouns:** Writing Resource Guide p. 9 Writer's Handbook p. 20
Singular and Plural Nouns	21	___ of 1	1 / 1	**Singular and Plural Nouns:** Writing Resource Guide p. 10 Writer's Handbook p. 20
		___ / 25	18 / 25	

Answer Key

1. C   2. B   3. D   4. A   5. B   6. D   7. B   8. B   9. A   10. D   11. D   12. A   13. B

14. C   15. C   16. A   17. C   18. A   19. B   20. B   21. A   22. C   23. D   24. D   25. C

THEME 6 Ongoing Test Practice

SAMPLE
Read the passage. Then answer the question.

Tula had a lot of big plans for the summer. She was going to go swimming at the town pool every sunny day. She also wanted to spend a lot of time with her friends.

S. Which sentence best synthesizes the information in this passage?

   A Tula did not want her friends to go to the pool with her.
   B Tula hoped that summer would be over soon.
   C Tula was going to go swimming and spend a lot of time with her friends.
   D Tula was excited about summer.

Read the passage. Then read each question. Circle the letter of the correct answer.

The Drive-In

"My family is going to a drive-in movie tonight," Gina said. "Do you want to come?"

"What's a drive-in movie?" I asked. "Is it a movie about cars?"

"No, silly," she answered. "It's a place where you drive a car into a <u>vast</u> field and then watch a movie on a huge screen at the other end."

"How can you hear what the people are saying?" I asked.

"You turn on the car's radio," she explained. "They play the sound from the movie."

It was the strangest idea I had ever heard. They did not have drive-in movies in the big city where I used to live. If you wanted to see a movie, you had to go to a theater. But things are different in my new town. I moved here about a month ago. There are a lot fewer people here, so there is a lot more open land.

That night Gina and I got in the car with her family and drove to the drive-in theater. They paid the woman at the gate and then found a good place to park. Some people were sitting in lawn chairs near their cars. A few yards away, some kids were playing tag.

Then the show started. It was a lot of fun. We sat in the back seat of the car and drank juice and ate crackers while we watched. When the movie ended, I thought the night was over. Then I found out that they were going to show another movie! I never saw two movies in a row at a regular theater.

When everything was over, all the cars pulled out and drove away. As we drove down the street toward home, everyone talked about how much fun it had been.

1. Read this sentence from the passage.

> "<u>Do</u> you want to come?"

Which of these words is a homonym of the word <u>do</u>?

- A don't
- B so
- C dew
- D can

2. Which of the following best summarizes the first two paragraphs of the passage?

- A Gina's family was going to a drive-in movie and she invited her friend to come along.
- B Gina invited her friend to go to a drive-in movie with her family, but he was confused because he did not know what a drive-in movie was.
- C Gina's friend didn't know what a drive-in movie was. He thought it was a movie about cars.
- D Gina asked her friend if he wanted to go to a drive-in movie with her family. Then he asked her a question about it.

3. What can you tell about the setting of this passage?

- A The passage takes place in a theater at a shopping mall.
- B The passage takes place in a large city.
- C The passage takes place in the fall.
- D The passage takes place at night.

4. What can you tell about the new town where the speaker lives?

- A The new town has more room, so it can have a drive-in movie theater.
- B The new town has only drive-in movie theaters.
- C There are more cars in the new town than there were in the city.
- D There is less room for people in his new town because the drive-in movie theater takes up a lot of room.

5. In this passage, <u>vast</u> means—

- A crowded
- B soft
- C narrow
- D huge

Answer the following question on a separate sheet of paper.

6. Using information from the story, explain whether you think the speaker will go back to the drive-in movies again.

THEME 6   Theme Progress Test

Read each question. Fill in the correct circle on your answer document.

1. When you write an essay, you should start with an introduction and end with —

   A an order
   B a transition
   C a description
   D a conclusion

2. Read this passage from "Key West, Florida."

   > Until the 1900s, people had to take a boat to reach the island [of Key West].
   > A state highway, built in 1938, connects the mainland with the island. The
   > highway includes one bridge that is seven miles long!

   Which sentence best synthesizes the information in this passage?

   A To get to Key West, you must travel on a highway.
   B People today would rather travel by car than by boat.
   C In the 1930s, people came up with a fast, interesting way to travel to
   Key West.
   D In 1938 a long highway was built to connect the mainland with the island.

3. Which of these words is a homonym for <u>loan</u>?

   A lone
   B borrow
   C lend
   D alone

4. What does the word <u>recreation</u> mean in the sentence below?

   > Now that all of our work is done, it is time for a little <u>recreation</u>.

   A things done to hurt other people
   B things done for fun
   C things done to help other people
   D things done for a job

5. Read this passage from a student paper.

> The lunch lines at our school cafeteria are too long. We have to wait a long time to get our food and pay for it. By the time we sit down, lunch time is almost over! We can make things better by having more people working at the cafeteria. We can also change the times that each class comes for lunch so the lines are not so long.

Which of the following best describes how the ideas in this passage are organized?

A plot and setting

B synthesis

C sequence

D problem to solution

6. Read this passage from "Mountain Homestead."

> The children's days were filled with chores and school. The <u>highlight</u> of every week was the day Father returned from the logging mill. He sometimes brought surprises, and he always brought money.

Based on the information in the passage, you can figure out that the word <u>highlight</u> means —

A first day

B best part

C last day

D worst part

7. Which of these is a homonym for <u>steal</u>?

A steel

B take

C borrow

D give

8. Which word in the sentence below is a verb?

> Clara gently stroked the kitten's fur.

A gently

B stroked

C kitten's

D fur

9. What are the two main parts of a story's plot?

A the characters and the setting

B the problem and the solution

C the problem and the setting

D the characters and the solution

10. What does it mean to synthesize information as you read?

    A use information in the text to help you figure out difficult words

    B predict what will happen next in a story

    C bring together pieces of information in a text to form a new idea

    D create pictures in your mind that relate to your senses and feelings

11. Which of these words is a homonym of <u>tow</u>?

    A push

    C two

    B pull

    D toe

12. Read this passage from the story "The Gigantic Redwoods: A Memoir."

> Beyond the canyon, the <u>massive</u> redwoods were visible from the roots to the branches. What an army of monsters! They nodded their lofty heads to the ocean wind that marched along the high land. They seemed to be a troop of giant soldiers climbing the mountain.

Based on this passage, you can figure out that the word <u>massive</u> means —

    A very thin

    B very quiet

    C very large

    D very windy

13. Read this passage from "Mountain Homestead."

> At that altitude the air was fresh, and the view was spectacular. Everywhere the family looked, they saw lush, green trees.
>
> The family got right to work. Father and Henry cleared enough land for the cabin. It was hard work. They cut down the trees and struggled to dig up the stumps.

Where do the events in this passage take place?

    A in a meadow

    B on a city block

    C in a small town

    D on a mountain

14. When writing an essay, when should you use a transition?

    A when you move from one idea to another

    B when you prewrite and draft

    C when you explain a thought

    D when you end the essay

15. Read these passages from "My A-mazing Summer Vacation."

> I really didn't want to go to Iowa. Of course, all I knew about Iowa was that the state grew lots and lots of corn, so I assumed I would be completely bored.

> My cousin and I got to work. First we gathered eggs from the henhouse; then we cleaned out the horse stalls. We took a break playing in the hayloft before we fed the goats and sheep. My uncle took me on his tractor and let me steer.

What can you tell about the speaker in these passages?

    A He does not like Iowa because he has to do farm chores there.

    B In Iowa he has to work hard, but he also has fun.

    C He learns that Iowa is exactly how he thought it would be.

    D He learns that Iowa is not as much fun as he thought it would be.

Choose the word that best completes each sentence for questions 16 and 17.

16. The farmer's crops grew very well this year because the land was _____.

    A vast

    B fertile

    C surroundings

    D recreation

17. When she looked in the mirror, she could see her _____.

    A reflection

    B horizon

    C farmland

    D altitude

Read this passage from "The Gigantic Redwoods: A Memoir." Answer questions 18 and 19.

> Early in our travels, we decided to see the gigantic redwoods. About two miles on our journey we began to wind our way upward around the side of a high mountain. The weather was hot. After the first few miles, the mountain was so steep that the children walked.

18. What problem do the characters face in this passage?

   A They do not know where the redwood trees are.
   B They are going in the wrong direction.
   C The mountain is too cold and rainy.
   D They are taking a difficult trip.

19. What can you tell about the journey based on this passage?

   A The mountain was the best place for viewing gigantic redwoods.
   B The travelers were going up the wrong path on the mountain.
   C The journey up the mountain was long and difficult.
   D The travelers had never seen gigantic redwoods.

Read this passage. The sentences are numbered. Answer questions 20 and 21.

> (1) Carla asked if she could borrow _____ math book. (2) Jim said that he would let her borrow his math book if he could borrow her jump rope. (3) Carla smiled and agreed.

20. Which word best completes sentence 1?

   A Jim
   B Jims
   C Jim's
   D Jims'

21. Which of these words from sentence 2 is a noun?

   A would
   B borrow
   C could
   D rope

Read this passage from "Key West, Florida." Answer questions 22 and 23.

> In the past, people in Key West made their living fishing. Today, tourism is the island's main industry. Deep-sea fishing and sightseeing boats dock at Key West's <u>port</u>. Key West hosts many boat races.

22. What does the word <u>port</u> mean in this passage?

    A a place where you park your boat

    B a place where you go sightseeing

    C a place where you can hunt for treasure

    D a place where tourism is popular

23. Which sentence best synthesizes the ideas in this passage?

    A If you go to Key West today, you can go deep-sea fishing or sightseeing on a boat.

    B Tourism has replaced fishing as the main source of money for people in Key West.

    C In the past, people in Key West went fishing to make some money.

    D Key West's main industries are tourism, fishing, and boat racing.

Read this passage from "Mountain Homestead." Answer questions 24 and 25.

> One evening, the family gathered outside the door to watch the sunset. "We've done well," Father said. "We have a roof over our head and enough food to eat. But we'll eventually run out of trees to cut and sell."

24. Which of these words from the passage is a verb?

    A evening

    B enough

    C sunset

    D gathered

25. Which new idea can you form when synthesizing this passage?

    A The family was happy with the life they had made.

    B The family gathered to watch the sunset every evening.

    C Father thought that he needed to fix the roof.

    D Father wanted to go out and cut down more trees.

Student _____ Date _____

THEME 6

Student Theme Progress Test Record

Skills Tested	Item Numbers (cross out numbers for items answered incorrectly)	Student Score	Criterion Score	If the student scored less than the Criterion Score, use these Reteaching Tools:
Comprehension Synthesize	2 10 15 19 23 25	_____ of 6	5 / 6	**Synthesize:** Comprehension Bridge 6
Use Fix-Up Strategies	6 12	_____ of 2	1 / 2	**Create Sensory and Emotional Images:** Comprehension Bridge 5
Target Skill Identify Plot	9 18	_____ of 2	1 / 2	**Identify Plot:** Teacher's Guide p. 180
Identify Setting	13	_____ of 1	1 / 1	**Identify Setting:** Teacher's Guide p. 191
Vocabulary	4 16 17 22	_____ of 4	3 / 4	**Vocabulary:** During independent reading time, review student's Vocabulary Journal and discuss how to improve the journal entries
Word Study Homonyms	3 7 11	_____ of 3	2 / 3	**Homonyms:** Sourcebook p. 169 Teacher's Guide p. 172
Writing: Process Writing Trait: Organization	1 14	_____ of 2	1 / 2	**Trait: Organization:** Writing Bridge 11
Organizational Pattern: Problem and Solution	5	_____ of 1	1 / 1	**Organizational Pattern: Problem and Solution:** Writing Bridge 12
Writing: Grammar Possessive Nouns	20	_____ of 1	1 / 1	**Possessive Nouns:** Writing Resource Guide p. 11 Writer's Handbook p. 21
Review Nouns	21	_____ of 1	1 / 1	**Nouns:** Writing Resource Guide p. 12 Writer's Handbook p. 20
Verbs	8 24	_____ of 2	1 / 2	**Verbs:** Writing Resource Guide p. 17 Writer's Handbook p. 23
		_____ / 25	18 / 25	

Answer Key

1. D 2. C 3. A 4. B 5. D 6. B 7. A 8. B 9. B 10. C 11. D 12. C 13. D

14. A 15. B 16. B 17. A 18. D 19. C 20. C 21. D 22. A 23. B 24. D 25. A

THEME ⑦ Ongoing Test Practice

SAMPLE
Read the passage. Then answer the question.

Paco lay in the grass looking up at the sky. The last thing he remembered was riding his bike down the big hill near the school. His left arm and leg hurt a little. When he sat up, he saw his bike about ten feet away. He was glad he decided to wear his helmet.

S. What happened to Paco?

   A He won a bike race.
   B He fell off his bike.
   C Someone stole his bike.
   D He decided to take a nap.

Read the passage. Then read each question. Circle the letter of the correct answer.

Mark Twain

Who is the best author in American history? A lot of people say that it is a man known as Mark Twain. His real name is Samuel Clemens. He was born on November 30, 1835. When he was only a few years old, his family moved to Hannibal, Missouri. This was a small town on the Mississippi River. Most of the business in town was connected to the river. Large boats stopped at this town to pick up and drop off goods that came from other cities and towns along the river. Many small boats also stopped there to buy food and clothes. This town meant a lot to Samuel. Many of the stories he wrote later in life take place in cities that were based on the town he grew up in.

As a young man, Samuel got a job working on one of the big boats on the river. He liked his job, but he wrote stories during his free time. He wanted to have a pen name. That is a fake name that authors sometimes use. But what name could he use?

Now the workers had to make sure that the boat stayed in deep water. If the water was too shallow, the boat could get stuck. It might even get a hole in it! So when the water in the river was about 12 feet deep, the men on the boat would yell, "mark twain!" This meant that the water was safe to sail in. Samuel liked the sound of those two words together, so he decided to make it his new name.

One of his most popular books is *The Adventures of Tom Sawyer*, which came out in 1876. It is about a boy named Tom and his best friend, Huck Finn. In 1882 he wrote *The Prince and the Pauper*. This story is about a prince and a common boy who look exactly alike. In the book, they decide to switch places because they each think the other one has the better life. Then in 1884 he wrote his most popular book, *The Adventures of Huckleberry Finn*. It is the tale of a boy who runs away from home and has adventures while floating with the <u>current</u> of the Mississippi River on a small, flat-bottom boat.

On April 21, 1910, Mark Twain passed away at the age of 74. Even though he has been gone a long time, his books are still read by people all over the world.

1. Why did Samuel Clemens set a lot of his stories in places that were like Hannibal?

   A He wanted everyone to go visit Hannibal.
   B He thought that all towns were like Hannibal.
   C He had happy memories of growing up in Hannibal.
   D He wanted Hannibal to be a very famous place.

2. Samuel Clemens is to boat worker as Mark Twain is to —

   A river
   B writer
   C Hannibal
   D store owner

3. What does the word <u>current</u> mean in this passage?

   A the flow of the water
   B a type of boat in Mississippi
   C something that floats on a river
   D the area where the river meets the land

4. What is a pen name?

   A a name a writer gives to a pen
   B the name of a town on a river
   C a name that is written down
   D a make-believe name

5. Why did Samuel Clemens call himself Mark Twain?

   A He did not think that Samuel Clemens was a good name.
   B Mark Twain was the name of a famous river boat captain.
   C He did not want to use his real name when he wrote books.
   D He thought people would not be able to remember his real name.

Answer the following question on a separate sheet of paper.

6. Why did Mark Twain decide to make *The Adventures of Huckleberry Finn* a story about a boy who floats down the Mississippi River on a flat-bottom boat?

THEME 7 **Theme Progress Test**

Read each question. Fill in the correct circle on your answer document.

1. Which word in the sentence below is a helping verb?

> Ericka and Jessica were practicing their new dance for the talent show.

   A were   **C** their
   B practicing   **D** talent

2. When you monitor understanding as you read, you —

   A look for hints about what will happen later in the story
   B stop and think about whether the information in a sentence is important
   C look for clues that will help you understand words you do not know
   D stop and think about whether you understand what you have read so far

3. Read this passage from "Typhoon!"

> "We're actually safer in deep water," Captain Li had replied. "If the sea gets very rough, we just have to point the ship's bow—the front—into the waves. That way, the ship will ride up one side of the wave and down the other. Picture how a toy boat acts on a lake when the water gets rough. That's a good [example of] what happens in a typhoon."

Which sentence best synthesizes the information in this passage?

   A Captain Li explained that the ship would be safer in deep water during a typhoon.
   B A boat in the ocean during a typhoon is like a toy boat on a lake in rough water.
   C Steering the boat into a wave will help protect it from damage during a typhoon.
   D Boats are safe in deep water when the sea gets rough.

4. Which of these words is a plural?

   A boss
   B shoes
   C less
   D grass

5. What does the word <u>analyze</u> mean in the sentence below?

> The doctor needed to <u>analyze</u> the X-rays before he could figure out what was wrong with the patient.

A pick up and deliver

B look at and study

C look up and explain

D lay out and measure

6. Read this passage from "The Vessel."

> The winking moon man looks down from the sky,
> Says, "Enough play, move on," and nudges it along.
> Crabs, clams, weeds, seeds, and shells from below
> Wash with it, under a star blinky sky, onto the powdery-soft shimmery [sand]
> The vessel waits to be plucked up, opened like a shell, its insides digested.

What is happening in this passage?

A The vessel is washing up on the beach.

B The vessel is being thrown into the water.

C The vessel is filling with ocean water.

D The vessel is drifting out to sea.

7. Choose the word that best completes the sentence.

> Walter and his father _____ the garage after working on a project.

A cleaner

B cleans

C cleaned

D cleaning

8. Read this passage from "Fighting Coastal Erosion: Why We Should Save Our Coastal Wetlands."

> Six feet a year might not sound like much. But those feet add up! Scientists warn that houses and other structures built within 500 feet of the water's edge are in danger in high erosion areas.

Which word best describes the speaker's voice?

A quiet

B concerned

C bored

D happy

9. Which of these lists contains words that are all helping verbs?

   A think, look, ask

   B could, some, big

   C see, walk, touch

   D have, would, can

10. Read this passage from "Making Waves."

> Fill the plastic bottle half full with water. Add one to three drops of food coloring to the water. Screw the cap onto the bottle and shake to mix the food coloring and water.

Why did the writer organize the information in the passage this way?

   A to tell you the most important information first

   B to let you decide whether the speaker is right or wrong

   C to show you the order that you should do things

   D to make you guess what is happening

11. Spring is to rain as winter is to —

   A shovel   **C** snow

   B January   **D** cloud

12. Read these lines from the poem "The Vessel."

> The vessel, a bottle, bobs on the waves,
> Like a dizzy kid on a carnival ride,
> Circling from cliff to cape to bay,
> Night upon day, flowing and floating and following the flotsam
> On an uncharted trip round and round.

Which word best describes the speaker's voice in this passage?

   A playful   **C** angry

   B worried   **D** sad

13. Which words in the sentence below are helping verbs?

> Rida will spend the summer at her aunt's house, which is located near Crystal Lake.

   A Rida, aunt   **C** the, at

   B will, is   **D** her, near

Read this passage from "Typhoon!" Answer questions 14 and 15.

> [Roberto and Marguerite] fought with the wheel to turn the ship toward the monstrous wave. Its movement was so <u>swift</u> that it seemed they could not possibly save the ship!

14. Why did Roberto and Marguerite try to turn the ship?

   A They thought they were lost.
   B They wanted to race with another ship.
   C They wanted to get a close look at a big wave.
   D They saw a big wave coming at the ship.

15. What does the word <u>swift</u> mean in this passage?

   A quick
   B careful
   C slow
   D mysterious

Read this passage from "Fighting Coastal Erosion: Why We Should Save Our Coastal Wetlands." Answer questions 16 and 17.

> Erosion is any process that moves bits of rocks and soil from place to place. Water, wind, and gravity cause erosion. Living things do, too. Oceans are the main force in coastal erosion. Waves, currents, and tides wear away the rocks and soil. Some of this material washes out to sea.

16. What does erosion do?

   A It prevents the ocean from flooding.
   B It makes mountains grow larger.
   C It keeps the wind from blowing too hard.
   D It causes land to slowly break apart.

17. Which of the following can cause erosion?

   A Taking a picture of some flowers.
   B Pouring water on a pile of dirt.
   C Mowing the grass in a field.
   D Swimming in the ocean.

Read this passage from "Typhoon!" Answer questions 18 and 19.

> [Marguerite and Roberto] heard the pilothouse door fly open and suddenly strong hands joined theirs on the wheel. Captain Li grunted as he fought to turn the ship. As the huge wave blocked the sight of everything else through the pilothouse windows, he finally turned the bow to face it.

18. What did Captain Li do?

    A He fought with Marguerite and Roberto over who would get to steer the ship.
    B He walked in and explained how to steer the ship safely.
    C He rushed in to help Marguerite and Roberto steer the ship toward the wave.
    D He ran into the room and yelled at Marguerite and Roberto for playing with the ship's wheel.

19. Marguerite and Roberto are to children as Captain Li is to —

    A mother
    B adult
    C brother
    D ship captain

Read this passage. The sentences are numbered. Answer questions 20 and 21.

> (1) Esteban is a kid who loves to play chess. (2) He meets some friends at the park every Saturday to play. (3) He hopes that someday he will become a great chess champion and travel all over the world.

20. Which word in sentence 1 is a linking verb?

    A is
    B loves
    C to
    D play

21. Which word in sentence 3 is a helping verb?

    A hopes
    B become
    C will
    D travel

Read this passage from "Typhoon!" Answer questions 22 and 23.

"How funny-looking!" Marguerite had laughed. But when she started to reach into the water, Aunt Pilar had almost shrieked.

"Don't!" she had cried. "Box jellyfish have a terribly painful sting," she had explained. "Some are even deadly!"

Aunt Pilar had told them that box jellyfish do not drift in the water like other jellyfish. They swim around, chasing food. They have 24 eyes. What's more, she had said, they have four brains!

22. Why did Aunt Pilar yell when Marguerite tried to put her hand in the water?

   A Aunt Pilar was afraid that Marguerite would get hurt.
   B Aunt Pilar did not want Marguerite to splash water everywhere.
   C Aunt Pilar thought that Marguerite was going for a swim.
   D Aunt Pilar did not want Marguerite to get her clothes wet.

23. Box jellyfish are to swimming as other jellyfish are to —

   A floating
   B sinking
   C diving
   D drifting

Choose the word that best completes each sentence for questions 24 and 25.

24. The rise and fall of the ocean is known as the _____.

   A current
   B coastline
   C shore
   D tide

25. A piece of pie is usually shaped like a _____.

   A model
   B wedge
   C chisel
   D current

Student _____   Date _____

 **THEME 7**

Student Theme Progress Test Record

Skills Tested	Item Numbers (cross out numbers for items answered incorrectly)	Student Score	Criterion Score	If the student scored less than the Criterion Score, use these Reteaching Tools:
Comprehension Monitor Understanding	2 6 14 16 18 22	____ of 6	5 / 6	**Monitor Understanding:** Comprehension Bridge 7
Synthesize	3 17	____ of 2	1 / 2	**Synthesize:** Comprehension Bridge 6
Target Skill Identify Analogies	11 19 23	____ of 3	2 / 3	**Identify Analogies:** Teacher's Guide p. 224
Vocabulary	5 15 24 25	____ of 4	3 / 4	**Vocabulary:** During independent reading time, review student's Vocabulary Journal and discuss how to improve the journal entries
Word Study Inflected Endings -*ed*, -*ing*, and -*s*:	4 7	____ of 2	1 / 2	**Inflected Endings -*ed*, -*ing*, and -*s*:** Sourcebook p. 213 Teacher's Guide p. 222
Writing: Process Writing Trait: Voice	8 12	____ of 2	1 / 2	**Trait: Voice:** Writing Bridge 13
Organizational Pattern: Sequence	10	____ of 1	1 / 1	**Organizational Pattern: Sequence:** Writing Bridge 14
Writing: Grammar Action and Linking Verbs	20	____ of 1	1 / 1	**Action and Linking Verbs:** Writing Resource Guide p. 13 Writer's Handbook p. 24
Main and Helping Verbs	1 9 13 21	____ of 4	3 / 4	**Main and Helping Verbs:** Writing Resource Guide p. 14 Writer's Handbook p. 24
		____ / 25	18 / 25	

Answer Key

1. A **2.** D **3.** C **4.** B **5.** B **6.** A **7.** C **8.** B **9.** D **10.** C **11.** C **12.** A **13.** B

14. D **15.** A **16.** D **17.** B **18.** C **19.** B **20.** A **21.** C **22.** A **23.** D **24.** D **25.** B

THEME 8 Ongoing Test Practice

SAMPLE
Read the passage. Then answer the question.

In 1961 a man named Alan Shepard became the second person and the first American to go into space. He went up in a ship called the *Freedom 7*. It was so tiny that he could barely move around. His flight lasted only 15 minutes, but it put him in the record books.

S. What question might you ask based on this passage?

   A Who went into space before Alan Shepard?
   B Who is responsible for putting things into the record books?
   C When was Alan Shepard's birthday?
   D What other important events in history lasted 15 minutes?

Read the passage. Then read each question. Circle the letter of the correct answer.

Would You Like to Buy a Raincoat?

Eric and Pang walked along the sidewalk by the river. They headed toward the large group of people standing just ahead. A loud roaring sound filled the air as the people leaned against the railing, looking down to the water below.

"I just love Niagara Falls," Pang said. "It's so beautiful here."

"We have a really great view from here," Eric added. "Look, I can see the water spinning around in a circle down at the base of the falls. When the strong, heavy water from the falls hits the still water below, they <u>combine</u> to form a whirlpool."

"It's like when you watch the water go down the drain in the sink," Pang noted.

The happy pair were on the American side of the falls. From where they stood, they could see a different country across the river. There were all sorts of stands nearby selling food, T-shirts, and raincoats. There was also a woman who tried to sell them tickets for a boat ride near the falls.

"I think we're going to climb down the path instead," Pang explained. "That way we can see the falls from the bottom."

"Oh, that sounds like fun," the woman said. "Can I interest you in some raincoats then?"

Eric knew that it was supposed to be sunny all day. "No thanks," he told the woman. So the two friends carefully made their way down to the base of the falls.

As they walked, a strong wind blew the mist from the falls against them. There was so much water that it was almost like it was raining. By the time they got to the bottom, they were soaking wet.

As they stood there dripping with water, Eric grinned and said, "I guess we should have bought raincoats."

1. What question might you ask based on paragraph 1 of the passage?

   A How many people were wearing raincoats?
   B When did Eric and Pang meet each other?
   C What is causing the loud roaring sound?
   D How long were Eric and Pang walking?

2. Which of these sentences from the passage contains alliteration?

   A *They headed toward the large group of people standing just ahead.*
   B *"I think we are going to climb down the path instead," Pang explained.*
   C *There was also a woman who tried to sell them tickets for a boat ride near the falls.*
   D *"It's like when you watch the water go down the drain in the sink," Pang noted.*

3. What does the word <u>combine</u> mean in this passage?

   A get wet
   B mix together
   C fall down
   D move apart

4. What question would you ask based on paragraph 5 of the passage?

   A What country is on the other side of the falls?
   B What kinds of food do Eric and Pang like best?
   C How much did it cost to buy a T-shirt?
   D How old was the woman selling tickets for the boat ride?

5. How do you know this story is realistic?

   A Niagara Falls is not a place that you can visit.
   B The events of the story could really take place.
   C You can really buy a raincoat at Niagara Falls.
   D Whirlpools do not exist in real life.

Answer the following question on a separate sheet of paper.

6. How would knowing about where the water goes in a whirlpool help you better understand what happens to water at the base of Niagara Falls?

THEME **8** Theme Progress Test

Read each question. Fill in the correct circle on your answer document.

1. When you write a story, you should always —

   A convince the reader to take an action
   B give your opinion about something in the news
   C explain how something works
   D include a beginning, a middle, and an end

2. Which word in the sentence below is an adjective?

   > The heavy rock broke loose and rolled dangerously close to the hikers on the mountain.

   A dangerously   **C** heavy
   B broke   **D** mountain

3. What does the word <u>artificial</u> mean in the sentence below?

   > Mr. Chang could not get any plants to grow in his yard, so he decided to put down some <u>artificial</u> grass instead.

   A fake   **C** wet
   B green   **D** seeds

4. What does the word <u>uncomfortable</u> mean?

   A very comfortable
   B not comfortable
   C too comfortable
   D to get comfortable again

5. How can asking questions as you read improve your understanding of a text?

   A Asking questions helps you figure out who the author is.
   B Asking questions helps you find difficult words in a text.
   C Asking questions keeps you thinking about your reading.
   D Asking questions keeps you from focusing on your reading.

6. Read this passage from "A Very Dirty Subject."

> Carla sat mindlessly watching an earthworm burrow its way into the soil. Closing her eyes, she whispered, "I wish I could follow you into the cool soil and escape this dreadful work."

Which words in this passage are adjectives?

A mindlessly, cool
B earthworm, burrow
C closing, whispered
D cool, dreadful

7. Read these lines from the poem "What Does Weather Do to Soil?"

> Gusts blow
> across the gravelly ground
> whipping dirt into storms
> turbulent soil rides the wind

Which line contains alliteration?

A *Gusts blow*
B *across the gravelly ground*
C *whipping dirt into storms*
D *turbulent soil rides the wind*

8. Which sentence in the passage below should be deleted?

> (1) Thomas Edison was a famous inventor. (2) He invented the light bulb in 1879. (3) His wife was a woman named Mary Stilwell. (4) He also invented the kinetoscope, which was one of the first movie cameras.

A sentence 1
B sentence 2
C sentence 3
D sentence 4

9. Which of the following words means *not friendly*?

A friendlier
B overfriendly
C unfriendly
D friendliest

10. What does the word <u>texture</u> mean in the sentence below?

> The pane of glass had a very hard, smooth <u>texture</u>.

A the way something smells

B the way something feels

C the way something sounds

D the way something tastes

11. Read this passage from "The Black Blizzard."

> Since he had been a toddler, Sam had heard about the Black Blizzard. Years ago, it had caused many families to abandon their farms and move away. At first, Sam thought it was a monstrous animal, like a giant black buzzard, that ate all the wheat and vegetables on the farm. Later, he understood more. The Black Blizzard was monstrous, all right, but it wasn't an animal. It was a huge dust storm.

What question would you ask based on this passage?

A Where did Sam live when he was a toddler?

B Where do giant black buzzards come from?

C What kind of monsters eat vegetables?

D Why did the Black Blizzard cause families to leave their farms?

12. What revision should you make to the sentences below?

> (1) He saw a strange shape in the corner. (2) He went over to look at it, and it moved. (3) His sister Carmela was hiding behind the curtain. (4) Tomas entered the bedroom and turned on the light.

A Move the first sentence to the end.

B Move the last sentence to the beginning.

C Switch the first sentence and the last sentence.

D Switch the second sentence and the third sentence.

13. Which list of words contains all adjectives?

A quickly, carefully, slowly

B person, bicycle, desk

C furry, strong, small

D sing, relax, listen

Read this passage from "A Very Dirty Subject." Answer questions 14 and 15.

As Carla repeated her wish for the third time, she felt her body slide below the dark, moist soil.

"It's lunchtime," said a voice. Carla jumped. The earthworm wriggled directly in front of her. "Feel free to snack on some soil, but I wouldn't recommend the rocks."

"What?" asked Carla in [surprise].

"Oh, you're a first-timer, I can dig it," the worm chuckled. "Get it? 'Dig' it?"

14. What question might you ask based on this passage?

   A How is it possible for Carla to slide below the soil?
   B What is the soil made of?
   C What will Carla's next wish be?
   D What time did Carla go outside?

15. How do you know that this passage is an example of fantasy?

   A Carla would not really repeat her wish three times.
   B Carla would not really be surprised by a talking worm.
   C Earthworms do not really talk.
   D Earthworms do not really eat soil.

Read this passage. The sentences are numbered. Answer questions 16 and 17.

(1) Jovita will be a professional tennis player someday if she practices every day. (2) Every morning she gets up early and walks down to the tennis court to practice. (3) There has never been a time when she woke up late or decided to take a day off. (4) She is the most dedicated person I have ever known.

16. Which sentence includes an example of future verb tense?

   A sentence 1
   B sentence 2
   C sentence 3
   D sentence 4

17. Which word from this passage is an irregular verb?

   A practices   **C** decided
   B walks   **D** woke

Read this passage from "The Black Blizzard." Answer questions 18 and 19.

> The dust kept coming, and there was no wheat to sell that year. Later, things got even worse. . . . Ma said the Dales, our neighbors, were going to leave their farm and move to California to find work. Pa said maybe we'd have to do that, too.

18. What question would you ask based on these lines?

   A Where was the dust coming from?
   B What kinds of food are made with wheat?
   C How long had the Dales lived next to Ma and Pa?
   D What is the capital of California?

19. Why were the Dales planning to leave their farm?

   A They wanted to move to a bigger farm.
   B They thought California would be a fun place to live.
   C They wanted to see what it would be like to live somewhere else.
   D The dust storms were making life too hard.

Read these lines from the poem "What Does Weather Do to Soil?" Answer questions 20 and 21.

> Sun shines down
> hot rocks swell
> icy night air chills the ground
> cold rocks shrink
> hot cold hot cold
> swell shrink swell shrink
> crack crash

20. What question might you ask based on these lines?

   A What are some different types of rocks?
   B Why do cold rocks shrink?
   C How hot is the sun?
   D Why is it colder at night than it is during the day?

21. Which of these lines from the poem contains alliteration?

   A *hot rocks swell*
   B *icy night air chills the ground*
   C *cold rocks shrink*
   D *crack crash*

Choose the word that best completes each sentence for questions 22 and 23.

22. When you move things apart, you _____ them.

    A layer

    B consist

    C combine

    D separate

23. Tiny bits of something are called _____.

    A particles

    B properties

    C textures

    D layers

Read this passage from "The Case of Vanishing Soil." Answer questions 24 and 25.

> The things in fertilizer that help land plants grow also help water plants grow. Water plants clog rivers and block out sunlight. When the plants die, they become food for bacteria. Bacteria use up oxygen in the water that fish and other animals need.
>
> I decided to use a natural fertilizer called *compost*. Compost creates fertile soil. It also will let me recycle my leftover coffee grounds, dead leaves, and torn up newspapers (brown materials). I can also recycle vegetables and grass clippings (green materials).

24. Why did the speaker decide to use compost instead of fertilizer?

    A Compost is less expensive.

    B Fertilizer can be harmful to nature.

    C Compost uses up less oxygen.

    D The speaker's green materials had become food for bacteria.

25. What question would you ask based on this passage?

    A How does recycled garbage fertilize soil?

    B How much coffee does the speaker drink?

    C What kinds of tree leaves can you put in compost?

    D What is the best way to unclog a river?

THEME 8

Student Theme Progress Test Record

Skills Tested	Item Numbers (cross out numbers for items answered incorrectly)	Student Score	Criterion Score	If the student scored less than the Criterion Score, use these Reteaching Tools:
Comprehension Ask Questions	5 11 14 18 20 25	____ of 6	5 / 6	**Ask Questions:** Comprehension Bridge 8
Monitor Understanding	19 24	____ of 2	1 / 2	**Monitor Understanding:** Comprehension Bridge 7
Target Skill Distinguish Fantasy from Reality	15	____ of 1	1 / 1	**Distinguish Fantasy from Reality:** Teacher's Guide p. 247
Recognize Alliteration	7 21	____ of 2	1 / 2	**Recognize Alliteration:** Teacher's Guide p. 256
Vocabulary	3 10 22 23	____ of 4	3 / 4	**Vocabulary:** During independent reading time, review student's Vocabulary Journal and discuss how to improve the journal entries
Word Study Prefix *un-*	4 9	____ of 2	1 / 2	**Prefix *un-*:** Sourcebook p. 243 Teacher's Guide p. 254
Writing: Process Writing Process: Revising	8 12	____ of 2	1 / 2	**Process: Revising:** Writing Bridge 15
Form: Story	1	____ of 1	1 / 1	**Form: Story:** Writing Bridge 16
Writing: Grammar Past, Present, and Future Verb Tense	16	____ of 1	1 / 1	**Past, Present, and Future Verb Tense:** Writing Resource Guide p. 15 Writer's Handbook p. 26
Irregular Verbs	17	____ of 1	1 / 1	**Irregular Verbs:** Writing Resource Guide p. 16 Writer's Handbook p. 25
Adjectives	2 6 13	____ of 3	2 / 3	**Adjectives:** Writing Resource Guide p. 21 Writer's Handbook p. 26
		____ / 25	18 / 25	

Answer Key

1. D 2. C 3. A 4. B 5. C 6. D 7. B 8. C 9. C 10. B 11. D 12. B 13. C

14. A 15. C 16. A 17. D 18. A 19. D 20. B 21. D 22. D 23. A 24. B 25. A

Mid-Year Review

Read the passage. Then read each question. Fill in the circle on your answer document.

Coney Island

How do you cool off in the summer when it gets really hot outside? Maybe you go for a swim in a pool. Maybe you go to a nice, cool movie theater or turn on a fan. If you lived near New York City 100 years ago, you might have taken a trip to Coney Island.

Coney Island is a piece of land by the ocean just south of the city. About 130 years ago, it was a fancy place where people went for a trip. They took boats and trains from far away to get there, and they stayed for days or weeks.

Then about 100 years ago, the subway came to the island. This meant that people living in the city could get there in just a little time. It only cost a few cents, and they could be back home by night. Soon thousands of people started going there.

Smart business people knew that the visitors to the beach would need something to eat. So they built a lot of food stands. You could get hot dogs, sandwiches, ice cream, and many other treats. They also knew that people would pay to have fun things to do, so they built amusement parks.

The Coney Island parks were the largest in the United States. They were known throughout the world. People came from many miles around to ride the roller coasters, the merry-go-round, and the Shoot-the-Chute. There was also a parachute drop ride. On this ride, people were lifted almost 200 feet into the air. Then they were dropped with a parachute that had a wire attached to keep them safe. Coney Island also had a giant Ferris wheel called the *Wonder Wheel*. The view from the top of this ride must have been incredible.

The most famous park at Coney Island was Luna Park. When Luna Park first opened, many places did not have electricity yet. Luna Park did. In fact, it had thousands of electric lights all over the park. It was probably <u>visible</u> from very far away at night. It's easy to imagine how amazing this seemed to people at the time. By all reports, it was a beautiful sight.

Luna Park also had animals. The most popular animal attraction was the trained elephants. It was not often that a child from the city got a chance to see a real live elephant.

After World War II, business started to drop. There were three fires at Luna Park. The last one was so bad that the owners had to tear the whole park down.

Also, more and more places in New York started to get air conditioning, so people could cool off much closer to home. More people also were able to buy cars. This meant that they could drive to other beaches that were not so crowded.

Other amusement parks started opening up in other parts of the country. People did not have to travel so far anymore to ride a roller coaster or drive bumper cars. In the 1950s, a big theme park opened in California. It soon replaced Coney Island as the major amusement park to visit.

You can still visit Coney Island today, but a lot of the old attractions are gone. Some burned down while others were torn down. New rides and parks were built to replace the ones that were lost. Not as many people come to visit anymore. But the beaches are still there, and you can still take a walk on the boardwalk and get a spicy sausage sandwich or sour frozen lemonade. Even though Coney Island has changed a lot over the years, most people say that the magic is still there.

1. Based on the information in the first paragraph, you can figure out that Coney Island was a place where people went to —

   A have fun
   B cool off
   C get hot dogs
   D see shows

2. What connection can you make between people in New York City in the early 1900s and people in New York City today?

   A Both have air conditioning.
   B Both go to Coney Island in large numbers.
   C Both like to go to the beach to get cool.
   D Both can visit Luna Park.

3. Using information from paragraph 5, you can figure out that the *Shoot-the-Chute* is —

   A a type of ride
   B something you eat
   C a popular show
   D an area on the beach

4. Which of the following best summarizes the last paragraph of this passage?

   A People no longer visit the beach because they have air conditioning.
   B Most people like the new attractions on Coney Island better than the old ones.
   C People don't visit Coney Island anymore because the old attractions are gone.
   D Some people still enjoy Coney Island for its history and attractions.

5. What does the word <u>visible</u> mean in this passage?

   A able to be seen
   B very dark
   C able to be heard
   D very high in the air

6. To figure out why people stopped going to Coney Island in the 1950s, you should ask —

   A What famous people were born in the 1950s?
   B Why did people prefer the park in California?
   C Why did people enjoy riding the bumper cars?
   D How far is California from Coney Island?

7. Which words in the last paragraph help you imagine how something tastes?

   A *rides* and *parks*
   B *attractions* and *magic*
   C *burned* and *torn*
   D *spicy* and *sour*

8. Read this sentence from the passage.

   > More people also were able to buy cars.

   Which word is a homonym of <u>buy</u>?

   A purchase
   B sell
   C by
   D guy

9. Luna Park is to amusement park as *Wonder Wheel* is to —

   A merry-go-round
   B shoot-the-chute
   C roller coaster
   D Ferris wheel

10. What is the main idea of this passage?

    A Coney Island was once a very popular place for people to visit in the summer.
    B Coney Island is a piece of land just south of New York City.
    C Coney Island used to be a place where people took vacations.
    D Before World War II, most places did not have air conditioning.

11. Read this sentence.

    > You could see things in Coney Island that you couldn't see anywhere else in New York.

    Which detail best supports this statement?

    A The subway came to Coney Island about 100 years ago.
    B There were thousands of electric lights all over Luna Park.
    C There are now amusement parks all over the United States.
    D After World War II, there were three fires at Luna Park.

Read the passage. Then read each question. Fill in the circle on your answer document.

Mum Bett

When was Mum Bett born? No one knows for sure. Her mother and father were slaves, and slaves were not allowed to learn how to read or write. This is why there are no records of her birth. We do know that she was only a few months old when she was sold to the Ashley family. This family lived far away from where she was born. After her <u>relocation</u>, the little girl never saw her parents again.

Mum was a slave at the Ashleys' house for almost 40 years. One of her jobs was to serve food and drinks to people when the family had a party. While she worked, she listened to what the guests had to say.

The United States of America was a new country at the time. A lot of people liked to talk about freedom and what it meant. They said that the new Constitution stated that all people were born free and equal. That means that no person is better or worse than anybody else just because of the family they were born into. This was a new idea for Mum. To her this meant that she could be free.

A short time later, she and Mrs. Ashley had a big fight. Mum got mad and left. She went into town to see a lawyer named Mr. Sedgewick. She told him that she had heard the people talking about freedom. She said that she should be free because she was born in America. Then she asked him to help her get her freedom.

After listening to what Mum had to say, Mr. Sedgewick decided that she was right. He helped her fill out the papers so that they could go to court. Brom, another slave who worked for the Ashleys, also wanted his freedom, so they added his name to the lawsuit. Soon their case went to court. In the end, the judge agreed with Mr. Sedgewick, and he set the two slaves free.

Once she was free, Mum changed her name to Elizabeth Freeman. She wanted her name to tell people that she was a free person and not a slave. She left the Ashley family and went to work for Mr. Sedgewick. She cleaned and cooked for him and his family and worked as a nurse, helping many sick people around town.

When Elizabeth Freeman died in 1829, she had many members of her family around her. One of them was her great-grandson W.E.B. DuBois. He grew up and followed in her footsteps. He fought for equal rights for African Americans just like his great-grandmother. The spirit of Elizabeth Freeman lives on in America today, where all people are considered equal.

12. What does the word <u>relocation</u> mean in this passage?

   A when someone is born
   B when someone gets a new job
   C when someone moves to a new place
   D when someone is sent back home

13. Why did Mum Bett need Mr. Sedgewick's help filling out the papers to go to court?

   A She never learned to read or write.
   B She did not understand one of the questions on the form.
   C She did not know where the court was.
   D She was not allowed to fill out the forms herself.

14. Which of the following is a theme of this passage?

   A A court is the best place to solve a problem.
   B All people deserve to be free and equal.
   C All people should be able to change their names.
   D Mum Bett was a brave woman.

15. Based on the information in the passage, you can guess that Mum Bett —

   A enjoyed working at the Ashleys' house
   B wanted to move back to the place where she was born
   C learned a lot by listening to the Ashleys' guests
   D thought that the Constitution did not apply to slaves

16. What connection can you make between Mum Bett and her great-grandson, W.E.B. DuBois?

   A Both fought for equal rights for African Americans.
   B Both were once slaves.
   C Both were taken away from their families when they were very young.
   D Both became free and changed their names.

17. Read this sentence from the passage.

   > A <u>short</u> time later, she and Mrs. Ashley had a big fight.

   What does the word <u>short</u> mean in this passage?

   A rude
   B not tall
   C not enough
   D not long

18. Based on the information in this passage, you can infer that —

   A Mum Bett did not like Mr. Sedgewick
   B Mum Bett felt bad about leaving the Ashley family
   C Mum Bett was much happier after she became a free woman
   D Mum Bett did not like to help other people

19. When do the events in this passage take place?

   A a short time ago
   B in the distant future
   C about 20 years ago
   D about 200 years ago

Read the passage. Then read each question. Fill in the circle on your answer document.

Spring Cleanup

Darnell and Shandi were sitting on the stairs in front of their apartment building. It was one of the first warm days of the year after the cold winter.

"What do you want to do today?" Darnell asked.

"I have no idea," Shandi said. "What do you want to do?"

"I guess we could go down to the park and shoot some hoops," he answered.

The two friends got a basketball and started walking down to the park. As they walked, they noticed that there was a lot of garbage everywhere.

"Look at this," Darnell said. "There are old newspapers, glass bottles, and other stuff all over the ground."

"All those things were buried under the snow all winter," Shandi said.

"Well somebody should clean this mess up!" he stated.

"I have a <u>solution</u>," she said. "We can do it. A lot of this stuff isn't really garbage anyway. It's stuff that can be recycled."

Darnell thought for a moment. Then he said, "All right, let's go home and get some trash bags. I didn't really want to go to the park anyway. I was just looking for something to do."

The kids ran back home and got some garbage bags and a large paper shopping bag with handles. "This job will <u>require</u> a few different types of bags. Let's put glass and plastic in the black trash bag," Shandi said. "Newspapers can go in the paper bag, and we'll put the real garbage in the white bag."

"Sounds good to me," Darnell replied.

They started on their own block, picking up the items left on the sidewalk and separating them into the proper bags. Before long, they had filled all their bags. They brought the full bags back home and got new bags. As they were getting ready to leave, Darnell's mother stopped them.

"What are you two doing with those bags?" she asked.

"We're cleaning up all that garbage outside, Mrs. Jefferson," Shandi said.

"And we're keeping the glass, plastic, and newspaper separate from the real garbage," Darnell answered. "That stuff can be recycled."

Mrs. Jefferson smiled and said, "I am very proud of you. The sidewalks are public property and we all should help keep them clean."

"We're doing our best," Shandi added with a smile.

The two friends went back to work, and soon they had cleaned up the whole mess they'd seen on their way to the park. Along the way, some adults saw what they were doing.

"Look at those kids over there," Mr. Lee said to his wife. "They're cleaning up all the trash in the street."

"Those children are real balls of energy," Mrs. Lee said. "They're doing such a great job out there. Why don't we get some bags and clean up in front of our store? It will look nice and more people will want to come in to shop here."

Mr. Lee went out and started cleaning up in front of his store. He even picked up the trash by the buildings next to his. Some neighbors saw what he was doing and decided to pitch in, too. Before long it seemed like everyone in town was outside cleaning up.

By the end of the day, there wasn't a piece of rubbish on any sidewalk in the entire neighborhood.

"What a long day!" Darnell said, wiping the sweat from his face.

"Yeah, but look at how much nicer everything looks," Shandi said. "And you know what? I had a lot more fun than I would have had playing basketball. It feels good to help the community."

20. Before they decided to clean up the sidewalk, what were Darnell and Shandi planning to do?

A go for a walk in the park
B play basketball
C visit Mr. Lee at his store
D make a snowman

21. Where in this story do you learn about the main problem the characters face?

A at the beginning of the story
B in the middle of the story
C at the end of the story
D in the title of the story

22. In paragraph 11, the author wants you to imagine what the different kinds of bags —

A smell like
B sound like
C feel like
D look like

23. What does the word <u>solution</u> mean in this story?

A the description of a problem
B the person who caused a problem
C the answer to a problem
D a way to avoid a problem

24. Read this sentence from the story.

> They started on their own block, picking up the items left on the sidewalk and separating them into the proper bags.

Which of these words is an antonym of <u>started</u>?

A finished
B began
C cleaned
D created

25. Which of these details is most important to the story?

- **A** Darnell's last name is Jefferson.
- **B** Mr. and Mrs. Lee own a store.
- **C** All the snow melted in spring.
- **D** There is garbage all over the sidewalks.

26. How is the problem in this story solved?

- **A** Darnell and Shandi decide to clean up the garbage on the sidewalks.
- **B** The sidewalks are clean at the end of the day.
- **C** Other people decide to help Darnell and Shandi.
- **D** Darnell and Shandi walk to the park.

27. Read this sentence from the passage.

> By the end of the day, there wasn't a piece of rubbish on any sidewalk in the entire neighborhood.

Which clue from the passage help you know what rubbish is?

- **A** The characters in the story live in the same building.
- **B** This story is set in a city in the springtime.
- **C** Many of the characters in the story have dialogue.
- **D** The characters spend most of the story picking up trash from the sidewalk.

28. Which sentence from the story includes a metaphor?

- **A** *The two friends got a basket ball and started walking down to the park.*
- **B** *"All of those things were buried under the snow all winter," she said.*
- **C** *"Those children are real balls of energy," Mrs. Lee said.*
- **D** *Before long it seemed like everyone in town was outside cleaning up.*

29. If you wanted to write a story like "Spring Cleanup," how would you organize your ideas?

- **A** from least important to most important
- **B** from most important to least important
- **C** from problem to solution
- **D** from solution to problem

30. What does the word require mean in this story?

- **A** something is needed
- **B** something is wanted
- **C** something is filled
- **D** something is found

Mid-Year Review

Extended Response Questions

1. According to the passage "Coney Island," why do fewer people go to Coney Island now than 100 years ago?

2. Using information from "Spring Cleanup," explain why Darnell and Shandi will probably continue to pick up trash they find lying on the sidewalk in the future.

Mid-Year Review

Writing Prompt

Most kids really like and respect an adult in their lives.

Think about an adult you really like and respect.

Now write to explain who the adult is and why you really like and respect him or her.

Hints for responding to the writing prompt:
- Read the prompt carefully.
- Use prewriting strategies to organize your ideas.
- Include details that help explain your main idea.
- Write sentences in different ways.
- Use words that mean exactly what you want to say.
- Look over your essay when you are done and correct any mistakes.

Mid-Year Review Test Record

Comprehension		Cross out numbers for items answered incorrectly.	
Make Connections	2 16	Use Fix-Up Strategies	3 27
Determine Importance	11 25	Synthesize	4 15
Infer	1 18	Monitor Understanding	13 20
Create Images	7 22	Ask Questions	6

If student has difficulty with Comprehension, use the Comprehension Bridges.   **Total Comprehension Score ____ / 15**

Target Skills			
Identify Story Structure	21	Identify Plot	26
Identify Theme	14	Identify Setting	19
Understand Metaphor	28	Identify Analogies	9

If student has difficulty with Target Skills, use the Teacher's Guide lessons.   **Total Target Skills Score ____ / 6**

Vocabulary

If student has difficulty with Vocabulary, review student's Vocabulary Journal.   5 12 23 30   **Total Vocabulary Score ____ / 4**

Word Study			
Synonyms and Antonyms	24	Homonyms	8
Multiple-Meaning Words	17		

If student has difficulty with Word Study, use Sourcebook and Teacher's Guide lessons.   **Total Word Study Score ____ / 3**

Writing: Process Writing

Organizational Pattern: Main Idea and Details	10	Organizational Pattern: Problem and Solution	29

If student has difficulty with Process Writing, use Writing Bridges.   **Total Writing: Process Writing Score ____ / 2**

Total Score ____ / 30

Answer Key

1. B	5. A	9. D	13. A	17. D	21. A	25. D	29. C
2. C	6. B	10. A	14. B	18. C	22. D	26. A	30. A
3. A	7. D	11. B	15. C	19. D	23. C	27. D	
4. D	8. C	12. C	16. A	20. B	24. A	28. C	

THEME ⑨ Ongoing Test Practice

SAMPLE
Read the passage. Then answer the question.

The oldest public school in America is in Boston, Massachusetts. It is called Boston Latin, and it opened in 1635. Students at this school studied art, reading, languages, and music. Students also had to study Latin.

S. How can you connect your school to the oldest school in America?

A Students still have to be able to play music to attend school.
B Students still have to take Latin.
C Students still study reading.
D Students still pay a lot of money to attend school.

Read the passage. Then read each question. Circle the letter of the correct answer.

The Interesting Tomato

Were you ever afraid to taste a food because it looked strange? Long ago, many people were afraid to eat tomatoes. That may sound strange, but it's true. People in Europe were afraid of tomatoes because they had never seen them before. They did not want to eat them. Some people even thought that tomatoes might make them sick.

The first people to grow tomatoes were the Aztecs of Mexico and the Inca of South America. When explorers from Europe first traveled to these new lands, they learned about many new plants. The Aztecs called tomatoes *tomatl*, which means "round and plump." The Aztecs called many other plants *tomatl*, too. The Europeans took these plants back to Europe in the 1500s. But Europeans <u>disliked</u> tomatoes. Tomatoes looked like fruit, but they did not taste like fruit. They tasted like vegetables, but tomatoes did not look like the vegetables these people knew.

We know now that tomatoes look like fruit for a reason. They are fruit! Tomatoes are actually large berries because they have seeds. A long time ago, the Europeans called all fruit apples. They called tomatoes apples, too. The Europeans planted these apples, but they thought they looked strange. They used them to decorate their yards because they were too afraid to eat them. When people from Europe came to settle in North America, they brought tomato plants back. People still believed the plants were harmful. Then in 1820 a brave American ate a whole basket of tomatoes. Some people thought the tomatoes would harm him. His <u>survival</u> surprised them. Soon tomatoes became a popular North American crop.

Today people grow tomatoes to eat, not to decorate their yards. People eat tomatoes fresh from the garden. They put them in many kinds of dishes. They make tomato sauce and tomato paste. They even make tomato pies. Once people learned how good tomatoes tasted, they were no longer afraid to eat them. People also use tomatoes in a variety of dishes because they are very healthy. Tomatoes are high in vitamins and help fight illnesses.

If you have never tasted a tomato, try one! You'll like it. Sometimes when you try foods you have never tasted before, you can be surprised how good they really are.

1. How have views about tomatoes changed over time?

   A People used to eat a lot of tomatoes, but today they decorate their yards with them.
   B People in Europe were the first to grow tomatoes, but then the Aztecs and Inca began growing them.
   C People used to put tomatoes in many different dishes, but today they only eat tomatoes fresh from the garden.
   D People used to think tomatoes were harmful, but today we know they are healthy.

2. What connections can you make between the Aztecs and Europeans in the 1500s?

   A Both took tomatoes to the Inca of South America.
   B Both used one word for many fruits.
   C Both thought tomatoes were harmful.
   D Both used tomato plants to decorate their yards.

3. What does the word <u>disliked</u> mean in this passage?

   A liked a lot
   B liked less
   C did not like
   D will not like

4. In this passage, <u>survival</u> means —

   A getting full
   B remaining alive
   C getting sick
   D being afraid

5. Which of these is most like a biography?

   A a book about the life of a European explorer
   B a diary of what a European explorer saw in South America
   C a story about how tomatoes got their name
   D a list of directions for growing tomatoes in North America

Answer the following question on a separate sheet of paper.

6. How have people's beliefs about tomatoes changed since explorers brought the plants to Europe in the 1500s?

THEME ⑨   Theme Progress Test

Read each question. Fill in the correct circle on your answer document.

1. The root word for <u>disobey</u> is *obey*. What does <u>disobey</u> mean?

   A to not obey
   B to always obey
   C to try to obey
   D to obey again

2. What does the word <u>surplus</u> mean in the sentence below?

   > Good weather this spring has resulted in <u>surplus</u> crops this fall.

   A higher priced
   B poor quality
   C many different kinds
   D more than enough

3. Which sentence has the correct punctuation?

   A I can't imagine what it is like to walk on the moon?
   B Dad shouted, "The astronaut landed on the moon!"
   C The moon travels around the earth!
   D The moon looks beautiful tonight?

4. Read this passage from "How the Crow Got Its Color—A Traditional Lakota Tale."

   > The great stampede shook the ground like an earthquake. The buffalo were fast and covered great distances in a short time.

   The author compares a stampede to an earthquake. What else could you probably connect a stampede to?

   A a train rushing by
   B a breeze blowing through the trees
   C a song playing on the radio
   D a dog barking

5. Which of these sentences would you most likely find in a biography?

   A To make a sandwich, you need bread, peanut butter, and jelly.
   B She was born on March 14, 1953.
   C Cows eat hay and drink water.
   D The eagle is the national bird of the United States.

6. Which of the following best describes a symbol?

   A a funny line in a story
   B a story that teaches a lesson
   C an object that stands for an idea or feeling
   D an object that is not real

7. What does it mean to make connections when you read?

   A decide the main point of the reading
   B write down words that you do not know
   C relate the text to other texts, your life, and the world
   D discuss the text with someone else who has read it

8. Read the sentence below.

   Mary prepays for her movie ticket.

   The prefix *pre-* in prepays shows that —

   A Mary does not pay for her movie ticket.
   B Mary pays for her ticket before the movie.
   C Mary pays a lot for her ticket.
   D Mary is the first person to pay for a ticket.

9. Which of these sentences contains a symbol?

   A Rabbits eat clover.
   B Clover is a plant with three leaves.
   C A four-leaf clover stands for good luck.
   D Clover plants have bright green leaves.

10. Which of the following would you most likely find in a biography?

    A ghost stories
    B the author's opinion
    C information about a country
    D facts about a person's life

11. What prefix do you add to the word *correct* to make it mean *not correct*?

A *dis-*

B *re-*

C *pre-*

D *in-*

12. Read these lines from the poem "Morning Light."

> Downy white feathers
> Are moving beneath
> The sunrise
> And along the edge of the world.

What question would you ask based on these lines?

A What time was the sunrise?

B What do the feathers stand for?

C Is the earth flat?

D How fast are the feathers moving?

13. Read this passage from "Sequoyah."

> Written messages could be carried across long distances without changing their meanings. Written records could be kept for years without being forgotten.

What connection can you make between written messages and the telephone?

A Both can carry information long distances.

B Sequoyah invented both.

C Both cost a lot of money to use.

D The telephone has replaced writing to record important messages.

14. Read this passage from "It's Only Natural."

> The native people of North America found many ways to meet their basic needs using the resources around them. They also used those resources to invent many useful items. Many people today still use these inventions.

What question might you ask based on this passage?

A In what year did Europeans first come to North America?

B What kinds of things did native North Americans invent?

C How did native North Americans hunt?

D What kinds of things do people invent today?

15. What prefix do you add to the word *fat* to make it mean *without fat*?

A *dis-*   **C** *pre-*

B *in-*   **D** *non-*

16. Read this passage from "How the Crow Got Its Color—A Traditional Lakota Tale."

> And so the crow escaped. But ever since, crows have had black feathers to remind them that the Lakota people need the buffalo to survive.

What are black feathers a symbol of in this passage?

A a reminder   **C** crows

B night   **D** a warning

17. Read this passage from "Sequoyah."

> Sequoyah's written system turned out to be very easy to learn. . . . The Cherokee realized how useful the writing system would be. Thousands of Cherokee people learned to read and write.

To connect this passage to yourself, you would think about —

A how many students attend your school

B how old Sequoyah was when he made his writing system

C how useful reading and writing are in your own life

D how many languages Sequoyah could speak

Read this passage. The sentences are numbered. Answer questions 18 and 19.

> (1) Thomas and Marie study history together. (2) History is _____ favorite subject.

18. Which word in sentence 1 is a verb?

A study   **C** history

B together   **D** and

19. Which pronoun best completes sentence 2?

A they   **C** our

B your   **D** their

Read these passages from "How the Crow Got Its Color—A Traditional Lakota Tale" and "It's Only Natural." Answer questions 20 and 21.

> The Lakota people lived on the prairies and depended on the region's buffalo for survival. They were respectful of their animal neighbors and never hunted more than they needed.

> Native Americans who lived on the East Coast of North America, like the Algonquin people, developed the boat called the birchbark canoe. . . .
>
> They used the <u>vegetation</u> around them to create their boat.

20. What connection can you make between the Lakota and Algonquin people based on these passages?

    A They both hunted buffalo for survival.
    B They both used nature for things they needed.
    C They both lived on the prairies.
    D They both used cedar trees for making clothes and homes.

21. What does the word <u>vegetation</u> mean in the second passage?

    A neighbor
    B a type of canoe or boat
    C plant life
    D an invention

Choose the word that best completes each sentence for questions 22 and 23.

22. There are very few cars left from the 1920s. Cars from the 1920s can be described as _____.

    A coastal
    B plentiful
    C scarce
    D population

23. Rivers, lakes, and oceans are all examples of _____.

    A vegetation
    B waterways
    C populations
    D plains

Read these sentences from "Sequoyah." Answer questions 24 and 25.

> [Sequoyah] listened carefully to the sounds of the Cherokee language. He created different symbols for each sound. After years of work, his system was ready. It was made up of 85 symbols. Each symbol stood for a syllable. The symbols could be <u>rearranged</u> to write down any spoken Cherokee word.

24. What connection can you make between Sequoyah's writing system and the English alphabet that you use?

   A Both have 85 symbols or letters.
   B Both are based on the sounds of the Cherokee language.
   C Both use the sounds of the English language.
   D Both use symbols or letters to make written words.

25. The prefix *re-* in the word <u>rearranged</u> means —

   A again   **C** after
   B before   **D** opposite

Student _____ Date _____

THEME 9

Student Theme Progress Test Record

Skills Tested	Item Numbers (cross out numbers for items answered incorrectly)	Student Score	Criterion Score	If the student scored less than the Criterion Score, use these Reteaching Tools:
Comprehension Make Connections: Text to Text, Self, and World	4 7 13 17 20 24	_____ of 6	5 / 6	**Make Connections: Text to Text, Self, and World:** Comprehension Bridge 9
Ask Questions	12 14	_____ of 2	1 / 2	**Ask Questions:** Comprehension Bridge 8
Target Skill Symbolism	6 9 16	_____ of 3	2 / 3	**Symbolism:** Teacher's Guide p. 291
Vocabulary	2 21 22 23	_____ of 4	3 / 4	**Vocabulary:** During independent reading time, review student's Vocabulary Journal and discuss how to improve the journal entries
Word Study Prefixes *non-*, *in-*, *dis-*	1 11 15	_____ of 3	2 / 3	**Prefixes *non-*, *in-*, *dis-*:** Sourcebook p. 269 Teacher's Guide p. 272
Prefixes *re-*, *pre-*	8 25	_____ of 2	1 / 2	**Prefixes *re-*, *pre-*:** Sourcebook p. 281 Teacher's Guide p. 288
Writing: Process Writing Trait: Editing	3	_____ of 1	1 / 1	**Trait: Editing:** Writing Bridge 17
Form: Biography	5 10	_____ of 2	1 / 2	**Form: Biography:** Writing Bridge 18
Writing: Grammar Review Verbs	18	_____ of 1	1 / 1	**Review Verbs:** Writing Resource Guide p. 17 Writer's Handbook p. 24
Singular and Plural Pronouns	19	_____ of 1	1 / 1	**Singular and Plural Pronouns:** Writing Resource Guide p. 18 Writer's Handbook p. 23
		_____ / 25	18 / 25	

Answer Key

1. A   2. D   3. B   4. A   5. B   6. C   7. C   8. B   9. C   10. D   11. D   12. B   13. A

14. B   15. D   16. A   17. C   18. A   19. D   20. B   21. C   22. C   23. B   24. D   25. A

THEME ⑩ Ongoing Test Practice

SAMPLE
Read the passage. Then answer the question.

Fairy tales are stories that usually describe some type of magic. They are told over and over again for many years. Sometimes they change a little over time. Many popular ones were written by the Brothers Grimm. The stories are fun to read and often teach a lesson.

S. Which information is most important if you are reading to find out where fairy tales came from?

A Fairy tales often include magic.
B Fairy tales have changed a little over time.
C The Brothers Grimm wrote many fairy tales.
D Fairy tales often teach the reader a lesson.

Read the passage. Then read each question. Circle the letter of the correct answer.

The Arrowhead

Carl and Sandra were playing hide-and-seek in the woods behind her house. When it was Sandra's turn to hide, she bent down behind a big rock. As she waited for her friend to find her, she noticed a funny-looking stone sticking out of the dirt. She dug it out and picked it up.

"I found you!" Carl yelled when Sandra stood up.

"Come look at this," she said. Carl walked over to see what she was holding.

"It looks like a triangle," he said.

"I think it's an arrowhead," Sandra replied. "My grandfather once showed me one."

"An arrowhead?" Carl asked. "What's that?"

"It's a stone that Native Americans used to put on sticks to make arrows," she answered. "My family is part Crow Indian. I bet my grandfather can tell us what it is."

The children took the stone to Sandra's grandfather. He looked at it closely and smiled. He told them, "Yes, this is a real arrowhead. This notch here at the bottom is where it was stuck to the shaft of the arrow. The tip is broken, so maybe the person who shot it hit something hard."

"How did it end up in the woods?" Carl asked.

"Long before there were any cities or buildings in this area, it was mostly woods," he explained. "There was no modern <u>civilization</u>. Back then, Native Americans lived here. One of our ancestors might have even made it, Sandra."

"Wow," she said. "Can I keep it?"

"I think you should," her grandfather replied. He went to a drawer and found a small box to put it in. Then he wrapped it in cloth so it would be protected.

Sandra took her new treasure home and placed it on her dresser. Every night before bed, she took it out of the box and looked at it. She tried to imagine the person who made it and what his or her life was like way back then.

1. Who is the main character in this story?

   A Sandra
   B Carl
   C Sandra's grandfather
   D The Native American who made the arrowhead

2. Which of these sentences from the passage best helps you figure out where Sandra found the arrowhead?

   A *Carl and Sandra were playing hide-and-seek in the woods behind her house.*
   B *As she waited for her friend to find her, she noticed a funny looking stone sticking out of the dirt.*
   C *Carl walked over to see what she was holding.*
   D *"I think it's an arrowhead."*

3. In this passage, <u>civilization</u> means —

   A new machines and computers
   B a place where arrowheads are made
   C advanced societies
   D people who lived a long time ago

4. Which sentence is most important if you are reading to figure out what an arrowhead looks like?

   A *"It's a stone that Native Americans used to put on sticks to make arrows."*
   B *He went to a drawer and found a small box to put it in.*
   C *When it was Sandra's turn to hide, she bent down behind a big rock.*
   D *"This notch here at the bottom is where it was stuck to the shaft of the arrow."*

5. Where is Sandra when she finds the arrowhead?

   A in the woods
   B in her bedroom
   C at her grandfather's house
   D at an archery range

Answer the following question on a separate sheet of paper.

6. What clues from the passage explain what Native Americans used arrowheads for?

THEME 10 Theme Progress Test

Read each question. Fill in the correct circle on your answer document.

1. What does the contraction <u>don't</u> mean in the sentence below?

   > I <u>don't</u> want to forget to bring my social studies book home after school today.

   A will not   **C** should not
   B do not   **D** did not

2. Read these passages from "My Park, My City" and "The Return of Ponce de León."

   > Could these be the trees Henry Hudson saw
   > As he sailed his ship up New York's shore?
   > These rocks I rest on with my friends—
   > Did Hudson also rest from his long passage here?

   > **Narrator:** In the early 1500s, the explorer Ponce de León sailed to Florida and claimed it for Spain. He now returns to start a new colony there.

   What connection can you make between Henry Hudson and Ponce de León?

   A Both sailed to New York.
   B Both were looking for land to claim for Spain.
   C Both sailed to Florida.
   D Both were explorers who traveled to America.

3. What does the abbreviation <u>Dr.</u> mean in the sentence below?

   > Mr. Chang lives at 643 Maple <u>Dr.</u> in San Antonio, Texas.

   A Doctor   **C** Drive
   B Mister   **D** Door

4. What does the word <u>foreign</u> mean in the sentence below?

   > A United States citizen must get a passport to travel to <u>foreign</u> countries such as Spain or Russia.

   A far-off   **C** unusual
   B very large   **D** unknown

5. Why is it important to understand your purpose for reading a text?

   A It helps you identify facts and opinions.

   B It helps you figure out the plot of a story.

   C It helps you determine the important information.

   D It helps you figure out what difficult words mean.

6. What does the word <u>cargo</u> mean in the sentence below?

   > When the ship sank in the harbor, nobody was hurt, but all of the <u>cargo</u> was ruined.

   A rope

   B automobiles

   C equipment

   D freight

7. Derrick is writing a letter. He wants to use the problem to solution organizational pattern. Which sentence best shows this pattern?

   A Math is a very difficult subject!

   B I was having a hard time in math class, so I stayed after class to work with my teacher.

   C There should be more math tutors at my school to help me study.

   D I understand math a lot better than I did before, but I still need to study.

8. Which contraction best completes the sentence below?

   > My aunt and uncle _____ sure if they will be able to come to the picnic on Saturday.

   A isn't

   B can't

   C aren't

   D wasn't

9. Read this passage from the play "The Return of Ponce de León."

   > **Ledesma:** Will we go ashore right away?
   >
   > **Ponce:** No. We must sail north along the coast to find the perfect place to start our colony.

   Where does this passage take place?

   A on a boat in the ocean

   B on a boat on a lake

   C on a boat on a river

   D on a docked boat

10. Read this passage from the poem "My Park, My City."

> Sitting on my perch in Inwood Hill Park
> I look, I see, and it seems to me
> The colorful leaves reflect on the water
> Like a jigsaw puzzle carefully put together.

How does the author let you know how she feels when she sits in the park?

A The author explains what her mood is that day.

B The author describes how she sees nature in the park.

C The author gives details about the other people in the park.

D The author talks about what she will do the next time she comes to the park.

11. What is the correct way to write <u>you are</u> as a contraction?

A you're

B your'e

C youare

D you'are

12. What is the correct abbreviation for <u>December</u>?

A Dr.

B De.

C Dec.

D Decem.

13. Read this passage from "Jessie Oonark: Inuit Artist."

> Jessie Oonark passed away in 1985. Her work is shown and sold at the Jessie
> Oonark Centre. The Centre is located in Baker Lake and shows Jessie's work.
> The Centre celebrated its tenth anniversary in 2002. It is also home to a
> group of Inuit artists who create art in Jessie's style. People around the world
> can still appreciate and learn about Jessie and the Inuit culture.

Which clue from the passage best helps you figure out what happens at the Jessie Oonark Centre?

A Inuit artists create art in Jessie Oonark's style.

B People around the world enjoy Jessie Oonark's art.

C The Jessie Oonark Centre is located in Baker Lake.

D Jessie Oonark died in 1985.

Read this passage from "Exploring the Explorers." Answer questions 14 and 15.

> I could see more of the ship than my last visit. The wood looked old and wet, and it was. Workers kept the wood covered with wet burlap to keep it from drying out and rotting.
>
> Dr. Liu, a historian on the boat, explained that this ship was in the bay only because Ledoux had become lost while looking for the mouth of the Mississippi River.

14. Where do the events in this passage take place?

A in a history class

B in a factory that builds ships

C near the Mississippi River

D in a bay

15. Which sentence best completes the chart below?

Problem	Solution
The wood was starting to dry out and rot.	?

A They put the wood out in the sun.

B They covered the wood with wet cloth.

C They poured water on the wood.

D They covered the wood with mud.

Read this passage. The sentences are numbered. Answer questions 16 and 17.

> (1) Kong and Mai lived with their parents in an apartment in Atlanta.
> (2) Every morning _____ wake up and have breakfast as a family.
> (3) Their mother _____ like eggs, but she makes them because Kong and Mai love them.

16. Which pronoun best completes sentence 2?

A we

B they

C them

D their

17. Which contraction best completes sentence 3?

A cannot

B can't

C don't

D doesn't

Choose the word that best completes each sentence for questions 18 and 19.

18. Every year we celebrate the _____ of the day my grandparents got married.

    A civilization
    B cargo
    C journey
    D anniversary

19. A _____ is a person who makes and keeps records about things that happened in the past.

    A explorer
    B historian
    C navigator
    D foreigner

Read this passage from "The Return of Ponce de León." Answer questions 20 and 21.

> **Ledesma:** *(surprised)* But surely, Sir, you can't believe the Fountain [of Youth] actually exists!
>
> **Ponce [de León]:** I only know what I heard from Columbus. A native guide told him about a fountain whose water helps a person stay young forever.
>
> **Miguel:** And if we find it, I'll never grow old!

20. Which sentence in this passage is most important if you are reading to figure out what the Fountain of Youth is?

    A *But surely, Sir, you can't believe that the Fountain [of Youth] actually exists!*
    B *I only know what I heard from Columbus.*
    C *A native guide told him about a fountain whose water helps a person stay young forever.*
    D *And if we find it, I'll never grow old!*

21. Which person is not a character in this passage?

    A Christopher Columbus
    B Ledesma
    C Ponce de León
    D Miguel

Read this passage from "Exploring the Explorers." Answer questions 22 and 23.

> In the 1600s, a Frenchman, Ledoux, arrived in our bay and anchored the ship. He went ashore to build shelter. A <u>bad</u> storm broke out and the ship sank, down through 18 feet of water, deep into the mud.

22. Which information is most important if you are reading to figure out how Ledoux's ship sank?

   A The ship was deep in the mud.
   B There was a bad storm.
   C The water in the bay is 18 feet deep.
   D Ledoux arrived in the 1600s.

23. Which word best replaces the word <u>bad</u> in this passage?

   A horrible   C naughty
   B wrong   D poor

Read this passage from "Jessie Oonark: Inuit Artist." Answer questions 24 and 25.

> Jessie was born around 1906. Her family lived in a community with other Inuit. The freezing temperatures made their lives hard. They fished for food. Whales and caribou—large deer—were important for food, too. These animals also provided materials the Inuit used to make clothing and shelter.

24. Which sentence contains the most important information if you are reading to find out what the Inuit ate?

   A *Jessie was born around 1906.*
   B *The freezing temperatures made their lives hard.*
   C *Whales and caribou—large deer—were important for food, too.*
   D *These animals also provided materials the Inuit used to make clothing and shelter.*

25. In what way has life changed since Jessie Oonark was a child?

   A People can now buy food in a grocery store.
   B People no longer go fishing.
   C People do not live in communities anymore.
   D People no longer need shelter.

Student _____ Date _____

THEME 10

Student Theme Progress Test Record

Skills Tested	Item Numbers (cross out numbers for items answered incorrectly)	Student Score	Criterion Score	If the student scored less than the Criterion Score, use these Reteaching Tools:
Comprehension Determine Importance: Purpose for Reading	5 10 13 20 22 24	____ of 6	5 / 6	**Determine Importance: Purpose for Reading:** Comprehension Bridge 10
Make Connections: Text to Text, Self, and World	2 25	____ of 2	1 / 2	**Make Connections: Text to Text, Self, and World:** Comprehension Bridge 9
Target Skill Identify Character	21	____ of 1	1 / 1	**Identify Character:** Teacher's Guide p. 313
Identify Setting	9 14	____ of 2	1 / 2	**Identify Setting:** Teacher's Guide p. 322
Vocabulary	4 6 18 19	____ of 4	3 / 4	**Vocabulary:** During independent reading time, review student's Vocabulary Journal and discuss how to improve the journal entries
Word Study Abbreviations	3 12	____ of 2	1 / 2	**Abbreviations:** Sourcebook p. 311 Teacher's Guide p. 320
Writing: Process Writing Trait: Word Choice	23	____ of 1	1 / 1	**Trait: Word Choice:** Writing Bridge 19
Organizational Pattern: Problem and Solution	7 15	____ of 2	1 / 2	**Organizational Pattern: Problem and Solution:** Writing Bridge 20
Writing: Grammar Subject and Object Pronouns	16	____ of 1	1 / 1	**Subject and Object Pronouns:** Writing Resource Guide p. 19 Writer's Handbook p. 22
Contractions	1 8 11 17	____ of 4	3 / 4	**Contractions:** Writing Resource Guide p. 20 Writer's Handbook p. 18
		____ / 25	18 / 25	

Answer Key

1. B   2. D   3. C   4. A   5. C   6. D   7. B   8. C   9. A   10. B   11. A   12. C   13. A

14. D   15. B   16. B   17. D   18. D   19. B   20. C   21. A   22. B   23. A   24. C   25. A

THEME ⑪ Ongoing Test Practice

SAMPLE
Read the passage. Then answer the question.

The first bicycle was built in 1817. The whole thing was made out of wood, even the wheels. This bicycle was not much fun to ride. It didn't have pedals, so riders had to push their feet against the ground to get moving.

S. Which sentence from the passage includes an opinion?

A *The first bicycle was built in 1817.*

B *This bicycle was not much fun to ride.*

C *It didn't have pedals, so riders had to push their feet against the ground to get moving.*

D *The whole thing was made out of wood, even the wheels.*

Read the passage. Then read each question. Circle the letter of the correct answer.

The Voyage of the *Half Moon*

Henry Hudson was an English explorer. In 1607 he set sail in a ship called the *Hopewell*. He and his sailors were looking for a fast route to Asia. They sailed near the North Pole but had to turn back because there was too much ice.

In 1608 Hudson tried again, but once again he failed to find a route. Even though he went a different way, he ended up in the middle of a lot of ice again. The blocks of ice hissed as they rubbed against one another. The sailors were probably frightened. They decided to turn around and sail home.

In 1609 Hudson went to the Dutch. He told them that if they gave him a new ship, he would find a faster way to get to Asia. They believed he could succeed, so they gave him the green light. They also gave him a new ship named the *Half Moon*. It was a much nicer looking ship than the *Hopewell*. At first he went north again. He ran into trouble and decided to try a different route. He sailed along the east coast of North America, taking notes about what he saw. He also made maps so that other people would be able to find their way.

Eventually Hudson found a large river that emptied into the ocean. He and his crew were very lucky. Hudson thought that the river might lead all the way to Asia, so he sailed up the river for many miles. He sailed from what is now New York City to what is now Albany before he realized that the river was not the special route he was looking for. So he turned around and went back to the ocean. He claimed the land he sailed through for the Dutch. Then he went back home.

Later the Dutch returned to Hudson's route and set up a colony called New Amsterdam. The Dutch played a <u>vital</u> role in the development of that part of the state. They also named the big river Hudson had sailed on the Hudson River in honor of him. Hudson must have been very happy.

Hudson sailed a few more times on a new boat called the *Discovery*. He found more bodies of water and mapped a lot more land. He was one of the greatest explorers in history.

1. Which of these sentences from the passage includes an opinion?

   A *Henry Hudson was an English explorer.*

   B *It was a much nicer looking ship than the* Hopewell.

   C *He also made maps so that other people could find their way.*

   D *Eventually Hudson found a large river that emptied into the ocean.*

2. Which word from the passage sounds most like what it describes?

   A hissed

   B notes

   C trouble

   D map

3. In this passage, <u>vital</u> means —

   A very important

   B not interested

   C very lucky

   D not valuable

4. Which sentence from the passage does not really mean exactly what it says?

   A *At first Hudson sailed north again.*

   B *Hudson thought that the river might lead all the way to Asia, so he sailed up the river for many miles.*

   C *He and his sailors were looking for a fast route to Asia.*

   D *They believed he could succeed, so they gave him the green light.*

5. Which of the following sentences from the passage can be proved true?

   A *The sailors were probably frightened.*

   B *Hudson must have been very happy.*

   C *He claimed the land he sailed through for the Dutch.*

   D *He and his crew were very lucky.*

Answer the following question on a separate sheet of paper.

6. Explain why the last sentence in the passage is an opinion.

THEME (11) Theme Progress Test

Read each question. Fill in the correct circle on your answer document.

1. Read this passage from "Meet Janalee P. Caldwell, Frog Detective."

   > Scientists are continually finding "new" species of frogs. Of course, the frogs
   > have been there all along. But scientists only find them when they visit areas
   > far away from cities. Every time I go to the rain forest, I find at least 5 to
   > 10 new species. However, I know I have barely scratched the surface.

   Which sentence from this passage does not really mean what it says?

   A *Of course, the frogs have been there all along.*
   B *But scientists only find them when they visit areas far away from cities.*
   C *Every time I go to the rain forest, I find at least 5 to 10 new species.*
   D *However, I know I have barely scratched the surface.*

2. What does the word <u>complex</u> mean in the sentence below?

   > Jerry was having trouble with the last problem on the math test because
   > it was so <u>complex</u>.

   A challenging
   B difficult to read
   C boring
   D easy to solve

3. Which statement best describes what a fact is?

   A A fact is something you do not agree with.
   B A fact describes a place.
   C A fact is a statement you can prove.
   D A fact explains how someone feels.

4. What can you do to make sure your sentences flow well from one to the next?

   A start every sentence the same way
   B use both long and short sentences
   C end every sentence the same way
   D make all your sentences the same length

5. Which word in the sentence below is a pronoun?

> Myleen asked the people at the table, "Would anyone like some carrot sticks?"

A Myleen   **C** table

B people   **D** anyone

6. Read this passage from the song "Sounds of the Rain Forest."

> The rain plops on flowers and branches,
> Some animals hide in a tree,
> Many will get wet and have fun,
> While others will sleep peacefully!

Which word from this passage sounds most like what it describes?

A plops   **C** wet

B hide   **D** sleep

7. What does the word <u>thrive</u> mean in the sentence below?

> Plants and flowers <u>thrive</u> in the rain forest because they get a lot of sun and water.

A die quickly   **C** grow well

B change colors   **D** need water

8. Read this passage from "Walking on the Tree Tops."

> On the damp rain forest floor, I take a deep breath to relax. Then I follow Dad.
>
> As we climb, I keep my eyes on the walkway. Dad calls out, "Hey Felicia! How much soup does a toucan eat for lunch?"

Which sentence in this passage contains an idiom?

A *On the damp rain forest floor, I take a deep breath to relax.*

B *Then I follow Dad.*

C *As we climb, I keep my eyes on the walkway.*

D *"How much soup does a toucan eat for lunch?"*

9. To write a persuasive essay, you must —

A tell the reader a story

B explain something that is happening in the world

C give the reader only facts

D try to convince the reader to do or believe something

10. Read these lines from the song "Sounds of the Rain Forest."

> As the lemur glides among the branches,
> The monkeys start swinging from tree to tree.
> Splish, splash, splish, splash, rat-a-tat-tat . . .

Which words from the song sound most like the things they describe?

A swinging, glides

B splish, splash

C monkeys, lemur

D tree, branches

11. Read this passage from "Meet Janalee P. Caldwell, Frog Detective."

> We do not have electricity, so we take enough batteries to use flashlights or headlights at night. We take lots of rice, beans, and dried cereal. We construct an open-air camp from small trees and use palm thatch for a roof. We hang hammocks to sleep in.
>
> The best thing is hearing all the frogs, insects, monkeys, and other animal noises at night.

Which of these sentences from the passage is an opinion?

A *We construct an open-air camp from small trees and use palm thatch for a roof.*

B *We do not have electricity, so we take enough batteries to use flashlights or headlights at night.*

C *The best thing is hearing all the frogs, insects, monkeys, and other animal noises at night.*

D *We take lots of rice, beans, and dried cereal.*

Choose the word that best completes each sentence for questions 12 and 13.

12. Every type of living thing is considered _____.

A an organism   **C** a nutrient

B a predator   **D** a zone

13. Animals that hunt other animals for food are _____.

A prey   **C** predators

B nutrients   **D** organisms

Read this passage from "Walking on the Tree Tops." Answer questions 14 and 15.

> "I love how the water sparkles," I say. "It's beautiful."
> "It looks even more impressive from way up in the canopy." He winks at me.
> I give him a shaky smile and try not to think about being up that high. . . .
> I wake up at dawn the next morning. Rain forest animals squawk and jabber around us as we eat breakfast. Suddenly, I hear a loud croak.

14. Which sentence from this passage contains an opinion?

   A *"It looks even more impressive from way up in the canopy." He winks at me.*
   B *I give him a shaky smile and try not to think about being up that high.*
   C *I wake up at dawn the next morning.*
   D *Suddenly, I hear a loud croak.*

15. Which word from this passage sounds most like what it describes?

   A moss   **C** forest
   B croak   **D** listens

Read this passage from "Tiger Talk: What Do You Think?" Answer questions 16 and 17.

> There's only one way to help tigers. We must save the land where they live. Large wildlife preserves offer safety for the animals. In a wildlife preserve, animals roam in their natural habitat. They hunt and raise their young on their own.

16. Which of these sentences from the passage is an opinion?

   A *We must save the land where they live.*
   B *Large wildlife preserves offer safety for the animals.*
   C *In a wildlife preserve, animals roam in their natural habitat.*
   D *They hunt and raise their young on their own.*

17. Which of the following details could you add to this passage to make it more persuasive?

   A the number of tigers living in the wild
   B what tigers hunt
   C how far tigers roam in their natural habitat
   D why it's important that we help tigers

Read this passage from "Walking on the Tree Tops." Answer questions 18 and 19.

> "And how high is this walkway?" I ask.
>
> "At least ten stories!" Dad answers. "The view is amazing."
>
> I try to look excited, but I'm terrified.
>
> "Look, Felicia," Dad points off into the distance.
>
> I follow his finger and notice dolphins jumping from the water in perfect semi-circles. "They're really cool!" I shout.
>
> "One is a gray river dolphin and one is a pink river dolphin," he tells me. "They live in the river."

18. Which sentence from this passage contains an idiom?

   A *"They're really cool!"*

   B *"One is a gray river dolphin and one is a pink river dolphin," he tells me.*

   C *I try to look excited, but I'm terrified.*

   D *"The view is amazing."*

19. Which of these lines from the passage states an opinion?

   A *"They live in the river."*

   B *"They're really cool!"*

   C *I try to look excited, but I'm terrified.*

   D *Dad points off into the distance.*

Read this passage. The sentences are numbered. Answer questions 20 and 21.

> (1) Nobody is _____ than my friend Omar. (2) He can make a joke about almost anything. (3) Whenever I feel unhappy, he just has to say a few simple words. (4) Before long, I will have the silliest grin on my face.

20. Which of the following words best completes sentence 1?

   A funny   **C** funniest

   B funnies   **D** funnier

21. Which word in sentence 3 is an article?

   A he   **C** simple

   B a   **D** just

Read this passage from "Tiger Talk: What Do You Think?" Answer questions 22 and 23.

> The tiger is one of the most beautiful animals in the world. Its orange coat with black stripes makes it one of the most unusual animals of the rain forest. The tiger is the largest predator of the cat family. The Siberian tiger can weigh up to 700 pounds! Tigers live in Asia. They hunt deer and wild pigs.

22. Which sentence from the passage is most important if you are reading to figure out what a tiger looks like?

   A *Its orange coat with black stripes makes it one of the most unusual animals of the rain forest.*
   B *Tigers live in Asia.*
   C *The tiger is one of the most beautiful animals in the world.*
   D *The Siberian tiger can weigh up to 700 pounds!*

23. Which of the following is an opinion about tigers?

   A *The Siberian tiger can weigh up to 700 pounds!*
   B *They hunt deer and wild pigs.*
   C *The tiger is the largest predator of the cat family.*
   D *The tiger is one of the most beautiful animals in the world.*

Read this passage from "Tiger Talk: What Do You Think?" Answer questions 24 and 25.

> Can zoos give tigers what a preserve can give them? Tigers need large areas of land to find food. Zoos do not give tigers large spaces to move around. In fact, you often see tigers in zoos pace around in circles.

24. Which line in this passage is most important if you are reading to figure out why tigers walk in circles at the zoo?

   A *Can zoos give tigers what a preserve can give them?*
   B *Tigers need large areas of land to find food.*
   C *Zoos do not give tigers large spaces to move around.*
   D *In fact, you often see tigers in zoos pace around in circles.*

25. Which of the following words from the passage is a pronoun?

   A tiger
   B you
   C often
   D find

THEME 11

Student Theme Progress Test Record

Skills Tested	Item Numbers (cross out numbers for items answered incorrectly)	Student Score	Criterion Score	If the student scored less than the Criterion Score, use these Reteaching Tools:
Comprehension Infer: Fact/Opinion	3 11 14 16 19 23	_____ of 6	5 / 6	**Infer: Fact/Opinion:** Comprehension Bridge 11
Determine Importance: Purpose for Reading	22 24	_____ of 2	1 / 2	**Determine Importance: Purpose for Reading:** Comprehension Bridge 10
Target Skill Recognize Onomatopoeia	6 10 15	_____ of 3	2 / 3	**Recognize Onomatopoeia:** Teacher's Guide p. 356
Vocabulary	2 7 12 13	_____ of 4	3 / 4	**Vocabulary:** During independent reading time, review student's Vocabulary Journal and discuss how to improve the journal entries
Word Study Idioms	1 8 18	_____ of 3	2 / 3	**Idioms:** Sourcebook p. 343 Teacher's Guide p. 354
Writing: Process Writing Trait: Sentence Fluency	4	_____ of 1	1 / 1	**Trait: Sentence Fluency:** Writing Bridge 21
Form: Persuasive Essay	9 17	_____ of 2	1 / 2	**Form: Persuasive Essay:** Writing Bridge 22
Writing: Grammar Adjectives: Comparative and Superlative	20	_____ of 1	1 / 1	**Adjectives: Comparative and Superlative:** Writing Resource Guide p. 21 Writer's Handbook p. 27
Articles	21	_____ of 1	1 / 1	**Articles:** Writing Resource Guide p. 22 Writer's Handbook p. 26
Pronouns	5 25	_____ of 2	1 / 2	**Pronouns:** Writing Resource Guide p. 19 Writer's Handbook p. 22
		_____ / 25	18 / 25	

Answer Key

1. D   2. A   3. C   4. B   5. D   6. A   7. C   8. C   9. D   10. B   11. C   12. A   13. C

14. A   15. B   16. A   17. D   18. A   19. B   20. D   21. B   22. A   23. D   24. C   25. B

THEME ⑫ Ongoing Test Practice

SAMPLE
Read the passage. Then answer the question.

Ryan's mouth was very dry, and his throat hurt when he swallowed. He crawled out of bed and stumbled to the kitchen to get a drink. As soon as the cool water splashed in his mouth, the pain melted away.

S. Which words from this passage help you imagine how Ryan felt?

   A crawled, stumbled, splashed

   B mouth, bed, kitchen

   C dry, hurt, pain

   D swallowed, splashed, melted

Read the passage. Then read each question. Circle the letter of the correct answer.

Lester's Report

Lester's hands were shaking and he had a funny feeling in his stomach. He looked through his notes again and again. One of his classmates, Becky, was standing at the front of the room. She was talking to the class, but Lester wasn't listening. He was just trying to get his thoughts together.

"Thank you, Becky," Mrs. Ali said. "All right, next up is Lester Adams."

Lester looked up quickly. He knew someone had said his name, but he didn't know who or why. Then he realized it was time to give his speech.

"Lester?" the teacher said. "It's your turn."

He nodded and gathered his notes. Becky passed by as she headed back to her seat. "Good luck," she whispered.

"Thanks," he answered. "I think I need it."

He wheeled his chair to the front of the room and turned to face his classmates. This was it. He gripped his papers hard in his hand. When he tried to speak, nothing came out. "What if I make a mistake?" he thought to himself. "What if everybody laughs at me?"

"Just relax," Mrs. Ali said from the back of the room. She could tell that Lester was as frightened as a mouse.

Lester took a deep breath and then let it out slowly. He remembered that the kids in the class were all his friends and that they would give him a fair chance. Suddenly, he was a lot more relaxed.

"My report today is on the Amazon rain forest," he said. He was surprised how easily the words came to him now. "The Amazon rain forest is located in South America. It is a very hot and humid place. Plants grow very well there. In fact, more than half of the plants in the world are found in this rain forest."

The more he talked, the easier the words seemed to come. As he looked out at the faces of his friends, he saw that they were all paying attention to him. He paused for a moment to smile. Then he continued. He talked about some of the different animals that live in the Amazon rain forest. He also explained how keeping the rain forest safe is <u>beneficial</u> to people all over the world.

When he came to the end of his report, everyone clapped for him. He couldn't help but grin as he rolled back to his desk. He had done it!

1. Which of these sentences from the story contains a simile?

   A *He knew someone had said his name, but he didn't know who or why.*

   B *He wheeled his chair to the front of the room and turned to face his classmates.*

   C *She could tell that Lester was as frightened as a mouse.*

   D *He talked about some of the different animals that live in the Amazon rain forest.*

2. How does Lester feel when Mrs. Ali calls his name?

   A He is scared because he does not know if his name has been called.

   B He is happy and excited that his name has been called.

   C He is angry and upset that someone has called his name.

   D He is surprised and confused when he hears his name called.

3. In the first paragraph, the author wants you to understand that Lester feels —

   A sleepy

   B nervous

   C curious

   D relaxed

4. What does the word <u>beneficial</u> mean in this story?

   A helpful

   B not helpful

   C expensive

   D not expensive

5. Which of the following best describes how Lester looks when he turns to face his classmates?

   A excited

   B bored

   C happy

   D scared

Answer the following question on a separate sheet of paper.

6. Using information from the story, explain how Lester changes by the end of his report.

THEME ⑫ Theme Progress Test

Read each question. Fill in the correct circle on your answer document.

1. Which adverb best completes this chart?

How	When	Where
carefully	late	?

   A nearby   **C** still

   B wisely   **D** always

2. Why is it important to create mental images as you read?

   A Creating mental images helps you locate similes and metaphors.

   B Creating mental images helps you identify adjectives and adverbs.

   C Creating mental images helps you picture the author.

   D Creating mental images helps you better understand what you read.

3. What does the word <u>eventually</u> mean in the sentence below?

> My younger brother was very short for a long time, but he <u>eventually</u> grew quite tall.

   A never   **C** finally

   B sometimes   **D** once

4. Which of the following is an example of how you would begin a business letter?

   A Dear Mr. Pennyworth:

   B I look forward to hearing from you soon.

   C September 8, 2007

   D Dear Grandma,

5. Which preposition in the sentence below gives you information about time?

> Ramona put her arms around her father and asked him to tell her a story about a princess before she went to bed.

   A around

   B to

   C about

   D before

6. Read this passage from "The Forest Has Eyes."

> Immediately my legs got tangled in a vine. Something burst through the bushes next to me. I had no time to get away. Curled into a ball, I shut my eyes tight.

Which detail best helps you picture that the speaker is afraid?

A The speaker's legs get tangled in a vine.
B Something bursts through the bushes.
C The speaker has no time to get away.
D The speaker curls into a ball.

7. What does the word <u>convince</u> mean in the sentence below?

> Megan tried to <u>convince</u> Henry to drive her to the mall, but she wasn't able to. He wanted to stay home and read a book.

A to remind someone not to do something
B to ask someone a question about something
C to tell someone not to do something
D to talk someone into doing something

8. Read this passage from "The Forest Has Eyes."

> We'd been deep in Brazil's rain forest for four days. So far I had seen the most amazing plants in the world. I had also seen incredible animals. I hadn't seen a jaguar, though, and I really wanted to. As far as I was concerned, jaguars were the real kings of the jungle. Lions don't even live in jungles!

Which of these sentences from the passage is an opinion?

A *We'd been deep in Brazil's rain forest for four days.*
B *I hadn't seen a jaguar, though, and I really wanted to.*
C *So far I had seen the most amazing plants in the world.*
D *Lions don't even live in jungles!*

9. Read this passage from "A Letter to Treetop Products, Inc."

> My class has learned that each day, hundreds of species of rare plants, animals, and insects are hurt by logging in the rain forest.

Which of the following words from this passage is a preposition?

A has
B in
C that
D and

10. Read this passage from "The Forest Has Eyes."

> It was a boy about my age. He must have been a member of the Yanomami. He stared at me. He didn't seem unfriendly—just *totally* serious.
>
> I didn't know what to do, but he did. He held out a hand and helped me up. Then he pulled back some vines and pointed. I could see our camp.

Which of the following sentences from the passage contains an opinion?

A *He held out a hand and helped me up.*

B *I could see our camp.*

C *He didn't seem unfriendly—just* totally *serious.*

D *Then he pulled back some vines and pointed.*

11. One way you can publish your writing is by —

A reading through it to find misspelled words

B reading it to your class

C reading through it to make sure your ideas are in order

D reading it to yourself

12. Which of the following sentences contains a simile?

A The snow covered the ground like a blanket.

B There had been a huge snowstorm the night before.

C John was excited to play in the snow.

D He and his little sister put on their coats and ran outside.

13. Read this passage from "The Forest Has Eyes."

> Just a few steps in, the foliage was so thick that I couldn't even glimpse sunlight. Pockets of mist hung in the air. The bugs and the birds made a nonstop screech.

Which word from this passage helps you imagine a sound?

A screech

B glimpse

C mist

D thick

Read these lines from "A Letter to Treetop Products, Inc." Answer questions 14 and 15.

> Cures and treatments for many illnesses have been discovered in rain forests. Did you know that twenty-five percent of Western medicines come from plants? The rain forests are like giant pharmacies!
>
> Does your company believe in maintaining one of our most important natural resources? If so, please send me information on how your company preserves the rain forest.

14. Which sentence from the passage contains a simile?

   A *Cures and treatments for many illnesses have been discovered in rain forests.*

   B *The rain forests are like giant pharmacies!*

   C *Does your company believe in maintaining one of our most important natural resources?*

   D *If so, please send me information on how your company preserves the rain forest.*

15. This passage comes from which type of letter?

   A personal   **C** business

   B friendly   **D** informal

Read this passage from "The Forest Has Eyes." Answer questions 16 and 17.

> Snakes were weaving through and over and into and under and among the trees. Something was crawling everywhere I looked—above my head, behind me, and under my boots. I thought I could feel insect legs skittering across every inch of my body. Then I remembered what my dad had said about the animals, and I could picture a thousand eyes gazing upon me hungrily.

16. As you read this passage, you can imagine that the speaker feels —

   A depressed   **C** curious

   B comfortable   **D** uneasy

17. Which of the following words from the passage is an adverb?

   A something

   B hungrily

   C skittering

   D animals

Read this passage from "The People of the Rain Forest." Answer questions 18 and 19.

> In many parts of the forest, the air is filled with the sound of bulldozers and the smell of burning trees. Experts say that if the destruction continues at the same pace, half of the Amazon Rain Forest will soon be gone!

18. What do you know about bulldozers that helps you imagine what's happening to the Amazon Rain Forest?

   A Bulldozers are large and are often used to destroy things.
   B Bulldozers are large and are often painted yellow.
   C Bulldozers are often used by construction workers.
   D Bulldozers have large black tires.

19. Which of the following words from the passage is a preposition?

   A be
   B the
   C at
   D if

Read this passage. The sentences are numbered. Answer questions 20 and 21.

> (1) Pablo carelessly left the door open when he went out to play in the yard. (2) His pet lizard, Iggy, immediately decided to follow him outside. (3) When Pablo saw Iggy walking around on the sidewalk, he ran faster than he ever had before. (4) He scooped up his little pal and brought him safely back inside.

20. Which word in sentence 1 is an adverb?

   A carelessly
   B left
   C open
   D play

21. Which word from the passage is an adverb that compares?

   A immediately
   B faster
   C safely
   D little

Read this passage from the poem "Gorillas in the Wild." Answer questions 22 and 23.

> [Gorillas'] long arms and hands help them move all around.
> They "knuckle walk" over the warm and wet ground.
> They love to take naps when it's time for a rest.
> Leaves, twigs, and branches are used for a nest.

22. In the first two lines of this passage, the writer wants you to picture a gorilla —

   A putting its hands on the ground as it walks
   B curled up in a ball as it sleeps in a cave
   C climbing a tree to look for some fruit to eat
   D taking a nap on the warm, wet ground

23. What feature does this poem have?

   A rhyming words
   B similes
   C an idiom
   D a symbol

Choose the word that best completes each sentence for questions 24 and 25.

24. An environment and the plants and animals that live in it make
   up _____.

   A bewilderment
   B an ecosystem
   C tropical
   D an interaction

25. A place that is very hot and humid is _____.

   A beneficial
   B ecosystem
   C improvement
   D tropical

THEME 12

Student Theme Progress Test Record

Skills Tested	Item Numbers (cross out numbers for items answered incorrectly)	Student Score	Criterion Score	If the student scored less than the Criterion Score, use these Reteaching Tools:
Comprehension Create Images: Enhance Understanding	2 6 13 16 18 22	_____ of 6	5 / 6	**Create Images: Enhance Understanding:** Comprehension Bridge 12
Infer: Fact/Opinion	8 10	_____ of 2	1 / 2	**Infer: Fact/Opinion:** Comprehension Bridge 11
Target Skill Understand Simile	14	_____ of 1	1 / 1	**Understand Simile:** Teacher's Guide p. 379
Recognize Rhythm and Rhyme	12 23	_____ of 2	1 / 2	**Recognize Rhythm and Rhyme:** Teacher's Guide p. 388
Vocabulary	3 7 24 25	_____ of 4	3 / 4	**Vocabulary:** During independent reading time, review student's Vocabulary Journal and discuss how to improve the journal entries
Writing: Process Writing Process: Publishing	11	_____ of 1	1 / 1	**Process: Publishing:** Writing Bridge 23
Form: Letter	4 15	_____ of 2	1 / 2	**Form: Letter:** Writing Bridge 24
Writing: Grammar Adverbs	1 17 20	_____ of 3	2 / 3	**Adverbs:** Writing Resource Guide p. 23 Writer's Handbook p. 27
Adverbs: Comparison Forms	21	_____ of 1	1 / 1	**Adverbs: Comparison Forms:** Writing Resource Guide p. 24 Writer's Handbook p. 27
Prepositions	5 9 19	_____ of 3	2 / 3	**Prepositions:** Writing Resource Guide p. 25 Writer's Handbook p. 28
		_____ / 25	**18 / 25**	

Answer Key

1. A   2. D   3. C   4. A   5. D   6. D   7. D   8. C   9. B   10. C   11. B   12. A   13. A

14. B   15. C   16. D   17. B   18. A   19. C   20. A   21. B   22. A   23. C   24. B   25. D

THEME 13 Ongoing Test Practice

SAMPLE
Read the passage. Then answer the question.

Gazing too long at the TV can hurt your eyes. When you look at something for a long time, it can cause eye strain. The next time you watch television, take a break every ten minutes and look around the room. Your eyes will thank you for it.

S. Based on clues in the passage, what does the word <u>gazing</u> mean?

   A staring
   B peeking
   C blinking
   D glancing

Read the passage. Then read each question. Circle the letter of the correct answer.

The 2,900-Year-Old Picnic

What do you think of when you think of a picnic? Maybe you think of eating food outside. Or perhaps you think of people tossing a ball back and forth in the park. You could probably come up with a million ideas. But no matter what you think of, there is most likely a picnic basket somewhere in the picture. You might be surprised to find out that people have been using picnic baskets for thousands of years.

If you go to northern Washington near the ocean, you will find a large forest. It is called the Olympic <u>temperate</u> rain forest. This is a kind of rain forest where the weather is sometimes cool and sometimes warm rather than always hot. A few years ago, some people were walking in the forest when they saw something strange. There was something on the ground near the edge of the snow line. When they looked closely, they saw that it was pieces of a basket.

The people picked up the basket parts and gave them to park rangers. They felt that it was the right thing to do. The pieces of basket were brought to some archaeologists. These scientists know a lot about Native American history. They often search for objects people used in the past. After studying the pieces for a while, they discovered that the <u>material</u> used to make the basket was about 2,900 years old!

The basket parts the people found came from a burden basket. This is a kind of basket that native people once used to carry things like fish and berries from one place to another. It is possible that the basket the people found once held food for members of a tribe who traveled away from home for a few days. If this is true, then that just might be the oldest picnic anyone has ever heard of.

1. Why did the people who found the basket give it to the park rangers?

    A The park rangers told the people that they had to give them the basket.
    B The people thought that they might get a reward for giving the basket to the rangers.
    C The park rangers asked them if they had found any old baskets while they were hiking.
    D The people thought that it would be wrong to take the basket home with them.

2. Which sentence from the passage uses exaggeration?

    A *You could probably come up with a million ideas.*
    B *When they looked closely, they saw that it was pieces of a basket.*
    C *The pieces of basket were brought to some archaeologists.*
    D *There was something on the ground near the edge of the snow line.*

3. Based on the information in the passage, you can tell that the word <u>temperate</u> means —

    A too hot
    B too cold
    C not too hot or too cold
    D too hot and too cold

4. What does the word <u>material</u> mean in this passage?

    A a kind of basket
    B what something is made of
    C something carried in a basket
    D where something is found

5. You can tell from the passage that a burden basket is used for —

    A holding papers
    B making a fire
    C finding a park ranger
    D carrying food

Answer the following question on a separate sheet of paper.

6. What can you tell about archaeologists based on the information in the passage?

THEME ⑬ Theme Progress Test

Read each question. Fill in the correct circle on your answer document.

1. Which suffix can you add to the word <u>bend</u> to make a new word meaning "something that can bend"?

   A -able

   B -ful

   C -less

   D -ness

2. Read this passage from "Lemons Against Cancer."

   > We'll sell lemonade at the School Fair on May 12th! The money we make will go to an organization that supports kids with cancer. Because I'm the class secretary, I'll keep a journal of our lemonade stand.

   You can figure out from the passage that a <u>secretary</u> is probably someone who —

   A makes lemonade to sell to people

   B sells lemonade to raise money

   C helps kids with cancer

   D keeps business records

3. Read this passage from "A Family Affair."

   > Our café has not been open for very long, but already it is earning money. That is important, because many businesses do not earn money for a long time. One reason we are successful is that I am a great cook! I bake all our cookies, muffins, and breads myself.

   Which sentence best completes this chart?

Cause	Effect
?	The café is successful.

   A The writer owns the café.

   B The writer is a good cook.

   C The café is open every day.

   D The café has not been open for very long.

4. Which suffix can you add to the adjective <u>glad</u> to make it a noun?

A -ness   **C** -tion

B -ion   **D** -ment

5. Which of these sentences includes a hyperbole?

A Mrs. Lopez wore a bright yellow dress to the concert.

B Tareq spent the whole afternoon doing his math homework.

C Paula ate a banana the size of a house.

D Mr. Lubov fixed the flat tire on my bicycle.

6. Prewriting is an important step in the writing process because —

A it gives you a chance to edit your work

B it helps you identify what your topic will be

C it is the time when you add details to your main idea

D it is the last thing you do before you finish your final draft

7. Read this passage from "A Family Affair."

> I knew I would need lots of money to start a business. So one day I took a big risk. I invested all the money I had saved. I gave it to a friend I trusted. To my amazement, he helped me double my savings!

By reading on in this passage, you can figure out that <u>invested</u> means —

A used money to buy something that you liked

B gave money to someone who really needed it

C gave money to someone in order to get more money back

D got money from someone who borrowed it from you

8. Read this passage from the play "The Shoemaker's Surprise."

> **LUCY:** Oh, I understand! Since Shoemart opened across the street, you have competition. You can't sell your shoes at a lower price, so you want to invent a shoe they don't sell. Then people might be willing to spend more money.

Which clue in the passage helps you understand what <u>competition</u> is?

A The shoemaker wants people to spend more money.

B The shoemaker can't sell shoes for a lower price.

C Shoemart opened a new store.

D The shoemaker wants to invent a shoe that Shoemart doesn't sell.

9. Which suffix should you add to the word <u>taste</u> if you want to describe something that has no flavor?

   A -able

   B -less

   C -ful

   D -ness

10. Ellen is trying to write an article for her school paper. She wants to use the cause and effect organizational pattern. Which sentence best shows this pattern?

    A Our school had a fundraiser.

    B For our fundraiser, we sold arts and crafts.

    C Our fundraiser was a success because so many students helped out.

    D We can find many good ways to use the money we raised.

11. The word <u>joyful</u> means —

    A not enough joy

    B a little joy

    C without joy

    D filled with joy

12. Which list contains words that all have suffixes?

    A celebration, kindness, employment

    B happiness, wonder, artwork

    C basement, loudness, waterfall

    D disrespect, unfriendly, misheard

13. Why is it sometimes helpful to read on past a difficult word in a text?

    A You can finish reading the text faster.

    B Only some of the words in a text are important.

    C It is good to keep reading even if you don't understand a word.

    D Clues in the text may help you understand the meaning of the word.

Read this passage from the poem "A Day for a Dollar." Answer questions 14 and 15.

> I'm put in a drawer but get yanked out again
> to make up the change for a neat, crispy ten!
> Then I'm stuffed in a pocket, exhausted and worn
> Where I'll nap forever. At least I'm not torn!

14. The writer uses words like *yanked* and *stuffed* to show that the dollar —

   A feels comfortable and relaxed
   B is being treated roughly
   C looks fresh and clean
   D is usually put in a wallet

15. Which line from this passage includes an exaggeration?

   A *I'm put in a drawer but get yanked out again*
   B *to make up the change for a neat, crispy ten!*
   C *Then I'm stuffed in a pocket, exhausted and worn*
   D *Where I'll nap forever. At least I'm not torn!*

Read this passage from "Lemons Against Cancer." Answer questions 16 and 17.

> **April 21** – The School Fair is only three weeks away! Today our class made a list of the supplies we need. Thanks to the donations from stores in town, we only need to buy sugar and ice.
>
> **April 25** – Today we painted a sign for the lemonade stand. We decided 75¢ per cup was a <u>fair</u> price to charge.

16. Based on the information in the passage, you can tell that <u>donations</u> are —

   A things given for free
   B lemons and wood
   C people in a class
   D things you buy at a store

17. What does the word <u>fair</u> mean in this passage?

   A expensive   **C** reasonable
   B cheap   **D** free

Choose the word that best completes each sentence for questions 18 and 19.

18. The money a business has left over after paying its bills is called the _____.

    A material
    B profit
    C inspiration
    D product

19. The things a company makes and sells are its _____.

    A profit
    B wealth
    C shabby
    D products

Read this passage from "A Day for a Dollar." Answer questions 20 and 21.

> Finally I'm picked up and given away.
> By a woman who takes me to the world's best café.
> She hands me over for a cup of hot tea.
> Where will I go next? What will happen to me?

20. Which clue from the passage best helps you understand what a <u>café</u> is?

    A *I'm picked up*
    B *She hands me over*
    C *a cup of hot tea*
    D *By a woman*

21. The lines "Where will I go next? What will happen to me?" help you see that the dollar —

    A is uncertain about his future
    B does not like hot tea
    C gets to choose what he will do next
    D wants to stay at the café

Read this passage. The sentences are numbered. Answer questions 22 and 23.

(1) Amelia carefully carries the eggs from the refrigerator to the table. (2) If she drops them on the floor, they will break and she will have to go to the store to buy more.

22. Which of these words from sentence 1 is a preposition?

   A carefully

   B carries

   C from

   D table

23. Which words in sentence 2 make up a prepositional phrase?

   A if she drops them

   B on the floor

   C they will break

   D she will have to go

Read this passage from "A Day for a Dollar." Answer questions 24 and 25.

They talk and <u>negotiate</u> on how to spend me.
What amazing toy will they buy? They just can't agree.
So instead they will save me and put me away.
Thank goodness—it's been an unbelievable day!

24. Which line from this passage contains a hyperbole?

   A *What amazing toy will they buy?*

   B *They just can't agree.*

   C *So instead they will save me and put me away.*

   D *Thank goodness—it's been an unbelievable day!*

25. What does the word <u>negotiate</u> mean in this passage?

   A discuss

   B agree

   C sell

   D save

Student _____ Date _____

THEME 13

Student Theme Progress Test Record

Skills Tested	Item Numbers (cross out numbers for items answered incorrectly)	Student Score	Criterion Score	If the student scored less than the Criterion Score, use these Reteaching Tools:
Comprehension Use Fix-Up Strategies: Read On	2 7 8 13 16 20	_____ of 6	5 / 6	**Use Fix-Up Strategies: Read On:** Comprehension Bridge 13
Create Images: Enhance Understanding	14 21	_____ of 2	1 / 2	**Create Images: Enhance Understanding:** Comprehension Bridge 12
Target Skill Understand Exaggeration and Hyperbole	5 15 24	_____ of 3	2 / 3	**Understand Exaggeration and Hyperbole:** Teacher's Guide p. 422
Vocabulary	17 18 19 25	_____ of 4	3 / 4	**Vocabulary:** During independent reading time, review student's Vocabulary Journal and discuss how to improve the journal entries
Word Study Suffixes -ful, -able, -less	1 9 11	_____ of 3	2 / 3	**Suffixes -ful, -able, -less:** Sourcebook p. 392 Teacher's Guide p. 404
Suffixes -ness, -ion, -tion, -ment	4 12	_____ of 2	1 / 2	**Suffixes -ness, -ion, -tion, -ment:** Sourcebook p. 404 Teacher's Guide p. 420
Writing: Process Writing Process: Prewriting	6	_____ of 1	1 / 1	**Process: Prewriting:** Writing Bridge 25
Organizational Pattern: Cause and Effect	3 10	_____ of 2	1 / 2	**Organizational Pattern: Cause and Effect:** Writing Bridge 26
Writing: Grammar Prepositions	22	_____ of 1	1 / 1	**Prepositions:** Writing Resource Guide p. 25 Writer's Handbook p. 28
Prepositional Phrases	23	_____ of 1	1 / 1	**Prepositional Phrases:** Writing Resource Guide p. 26 Writer's Handbook p. 28
		_____ / 25	18 / 25	

Answer Key

1. A   2. D   3. B   4. A   5. C   6. B   7. C   8. D   9. B   10. C   11. D   12. A   13. D

14. B   15. D   16. A   17. C   18. B   19. D   20. C   21. A   22. C   23. B   24. D   25. A

THEME ⑭ Ongoing Test Practice

SAMPLE
Read the passage. Then answer the question.

The first sneaker was invented in 1893. It was made of canvas. The inventor wanted to make a shoe for boaters so they did not have to wear dress shoes on the deck. Dress shoes are often made of leather and are more formal. People wear them when they dress up.

S. What do sneakers and dress shoes have in common?

    A They are both made of canvas.
    B They both protect your feet.
    C They were both invented in 1893.
    D They are both formal types of shoes.

Read the passage. Then read each question. Circle the letter of the correct answer.

Grandma's Orange Juice

Jeff and Mary burst through the back door of their grandmother's house and ran to the refrigerator. They had been playing outside all morning. First they went swimming and then they played tag. After that, they rode bikes up and down the driveway. By the time they came inside, they were really thirsty.

"There's water, milk, and orange juice," Mary stated. "What should we have?"

"Grandma's orange juice!" Jeff answered. "She makes the best juice I've ever had!"

Mary carefully took out the pitcher of juice and set it on the counter. Her brother went into the cabinet and pulled out two cups. They each poured some juice and drank it down quickly.

"My, my, somebody's thirsty out here," Grandma said as she entered the kitchen. "Now be careful not to drink too much or else your skin might turn orange."

"You make the best orange juice ever, Grandma," Jeff said.

"I suggest that you sell it," Mary added. "I bet you would make a whole lot of money!"

Jeff said, "I don't think she should sell it. I'd rather get it here for free!"

Grandma laughed. "Do you want to know what makes my juice so good?" she asked. "Regular orange juice is made just from oranges. I use a few different fruits to make mine. First I squeeze the juice from five or six oranges into a pitcher.

Then I drain the juice out of a grapefruit to add a sour flavor. Next I take a handful of strawberries and put them in the blender. After letting the blender run for a minute, I turn it off and pour the strawberry pieces into the pitcher, too. Then I add some water and stir in a little sugar."

"That's a lot of fruit," Jeff said. "No wonder it's so delicious."

"But can you guess the most important ingredient I put in my juice?" she asked.

"Cherries?" Mary asked.

"Apples?" Jeff guessed.

"No," Grandma replied. "The most important ingredient is love."

1. Read this sentence from the story.

> Mary <u>carefully</u> took out the pitcher of juice and set it on the counter.

What does the word <u>carefully</u> mean?

A without care

B not enough care

C in need of care

D with great care

2. What does the word <u>suggest</u> mean in this passage?

A to give advice

B to force someone

C to refuse to do what is asked

D to take something away

3. What does Grandma put in her juice to make it taste sweet?

A water and grapefruit juice

B grapefruit juice and cherries

C strawberries and sugar

D cherries and apples

4. Both Jeff and Mary —

A want Grandma to start her own orange juice business

B think Grandma might put apples in her juice

C love the flavor of Grandma's orange juice

D worry that they might have to pay for Grandma's juice

5. Which line from the story is meant to make you smile or laugh?

A *They had been playing outside all morning.*

B *"Now be careful not to drink too much or else your skin might turn orange."*

C *"You make the best orange juice ever, Grandma."*

D *"Do you want to know what makes my juice so good?"*

Answer the following question on a separate sheet of paper.

6. Using information from the passage, explain how Grandma's orange juice is different from regular orange juice.

THEME 14 Theme Progress Test

Read each question. Fill in the correct circle on your answer document.

1. What does it mean to classify and categorize the information you read?

   A look for words and phrases that do not really mean what they say

   B figure out whether a statement is fact or opinion

   C use clues in a passage to figure out what the writer wants you to imagine

   D put words or ideas that have something in common into groups

2. Which word in the sentence below is a conjunction?

   > We had planned to go to the library together on Saturday afternoon, but poor Aura got sick and could not go.

   A we

   B together

   C but

   D could

3. Read this passage from "Buy! Buy! Why?"

   > TV isn't the only place advertisers place ads to reach you. Ads shout from the radio. They jump out at you from billboards. They're waiting on Internet pages and in movies. Sometimes, they're even hiding in the video games you play.

   Which set of words best completes this chart?

Ads you can hear	Ads you must read
TV and radio	?

   A billboards and Internet pages

   B video games and radio

   C billboards and radio

   D Internet pages and TV

4. The word <u>hopefully</u> means —

   A with not enough hope   **C** with great hope

   B with too much hope   **D** without hope

5. If you <u>recommend</u> that Karen buys a hat, you —

    A ask her not to buy a hat   **C** buy a hat for her

    B urge her to buy a hat   **D** tell her not to buy a hat

6. Which sentence is written correctly?

    A do not pour too much water into the vase.

    B Who is knocking on the front door!

    C Peter felled lucky when he found a penny on the sidewalk

    D Margaret had a great time playing basketball in the park.

7. Which conjunction best completes the sentence below?

> Would you rather see the monster movie _____ the movie about the tennis player?

    A but

    B or

    C and

    D either

8. Read these lines from the song "Hot Cross Buns."

> If you have no daughters,
> Give them to your sons!
> One-a-penny,
> Two-a-penny,
> Hot cross buns!

Why does the writer say "If you have no daughters, Give them to your sons"?

    A to help you imagine how the buns taste

    B to explain why people like hot cross buns

    C to make you smile

    D to make you feel sad

9. What suffix do you add to the word <u>silent</u> to make it mean "in a silent way"?

    A -less

    B -able

    C -fully

    D -ly

10. Read this passage from "Buy! Buy! Why?"

> Companies want you to buy food, electronics, toys, and other items. They want to get your hard-earned allowance and babysitting dollars. They try to reach you in many ways, including TV, movies, video games, print ads, and the Internet.

Which word best completes this chart?

Things Companies Want You to Buy	Ways Companies Try to Get Your Attention
food	print ads
toys	video games
electronics	?

A movies

B allowance

C babysitting

D dollars

11. Which sentence is written correctly?

A Do you remember where I put my keys.

B Aria shouted "Here I am."

C What time does your sister's soccer game start?

D "Rachel said, Let's go to the mall after school."

12. Read this passage from "Buy! Buy! Why?"

> Imagine you're racing a car down the track in a video game. You screech around a corner and just miss running into a billboard—a billboard for a fast food restaurant. You speedily make it to the finish line. Flags wave to show that you finished in first place. The flags show the logo of a popular running shoe.

In what way are the flags similar to the billboard in this passage?

A They both have the name of a running shoe on them.

B They both have the name of a restaurant on them.

C They both show you won the game.

D They are both kinds of advertisements.

13. Which conjunction best completes the sentence below?

> Amy wants to go out with her friends, _____ she feels like she should stay home and spend some time with her grandmother.

   A or   **C** either

   B yet   **D** and

Read this passage from "The Two Merchants." Answer questions 14 and 15.

> "Well," said Ochen, with a mischievous twinkle in his eye, "I don't have any money, but how about a trade? I can trade you this fine cloth for your ants. It's the most beautiful piece I have," Ochen told Akello. "I'm giving you a pretty good <u>bargain</u> if you ask me."
>
> "OK," Akello answered, "Let's trade."
>
> Akello gave the ant wings to Ochen. Ochen gave the rags to Akello.

14. Based on the information in this passage, you can figure out that Ochen had a mischievous twinkle in his eye because —

   A he thought he was tricking Akello

   B he thought that Akello was tricking him

   C he did not want Akello to get his rags

   D he believed that his rags were really fine cloth

15. What is the meaning of the word <u>bargain</u>?

   A a kind of money   **C** a beautiful cloth

   B a good deal   **D** a tasty type of ant

Choose the word that best completes each sentence for questions 16 and 17.

16. When two people agree to give up something they want in order to get something from the other person, they come to a _____.

   A compromise   **C** bargain

   B merchant   **D** brim

17. The amount of items that a store has available to sell is called its _____.

   A bargain   **C** demand

   B purchase   **D** supply

Read this passage from "The Two Merchants." Answer questions 18 and 19.

[Akello and Ochen] set up tents for shade. All around them, other [people] laid out goods for sale. Akello waited for someone to buy his ant wings, and Ochen waited for someone to buy his bundle of rags. The noisy and bustling market was full of people. . . .

Children laughed and ran among the different [people selling things]. Their parents carried baskets full of food and clothes.

18. How are Akello and Ochen alike?

   A Akello and Ochen sell things and sit in the shade.
   B Akello and Ochen buy things and sit in the shade.
   C Akello and Ochen sell things and sit in the sun.
   D Akello and Ochen buy things and sit in the sun.

19. Based on the clues in the passage, you can figure out that <u>bustling</u> means —

   A hushed   **C** busy
   B colorful   **D** dull

Read these lines from the song "Paperboy's Song." Answer questions 20 and 21.

Headlines! Headlines!
Read all about it.
Defeated candidate tells country:
"I quit!"

Headlines! Headlines!
You heard it here first.

20. Which information in this passage is not meant to be taken seriously?

   A *You heard it here first.*
   B *Read all about it.*
   C *Defeated candidate tells country: "I quit!"*
   D *Headlines! Headlines!*

21. How is this song similar to a poem?

   A It talks about many different characters.
   B It has a rhythm when you read it.
   C All of the words in the passage rhyme.
   D It gives facts about the real world.

Read this passage from the poem "Sunday at the Farmers' Market."
Answer questions 22 and 23.

> Potatoes, plums, and pumpkins, too,
> Piping hot bread and vegetable stew
> All at the farmers' market.
>
> Find carrots fresh, and berries ripe,
> As for lettuce, there's every type
> All at the farmers' market.

22. What do all of the foods in this poem have in common?

   A They are all fruit.
   B They are all vegetables.
   C They all come from farms.
   D They are all piping hot.

23. Why does the writer repeat the line "All at the farmer's market" in the poem?

   A to give the poem rhythm
   B because the last word in every line rhymes with "market"
   C to make the reader want to go shopping
   D to help the reader imagine what the market sounds like

Read this passage. The sentences are numbered. Answer questions
24 and 25.

> (1) The kids in the music club want to go see a concert, _____ the kids
> in the drama club want to go see a play. (2) _____ we decide which one
> to go to, _____ we will not go on a field trip at all.

24. Which conjunction best completes sentence 1?

   A or   C either
   B and   D so

25. Which set of conjunctions best completes sentence 2?

   A either, and   C both, and
   B both, or   D either, or

THEME 14

Student Theme Progress Test Record

Skills Tested	Item Numbers (cross out numbers for items answered incorrectly)	Student Score	Criterion Score	If the student scored less than the Criterion Score, use these Reteaching Tools:
Comprehension Synthesize: Classify and Categorize Information	1 3 10 12 18 22	___ of 6	5 / 6	**Synthesize: Classify and Categorize Information:** Comprehension Bridge 14
Use Fix-Up Strategies: Read on	14 19	___ of 2	1 / 2	**Use Fix-Up Strategies: Read on:** Comprehension Bridge 13
Target Skill Identify Repetition	23	___ of 1	1 / 1	**Identify Repetition:** Teacher's Guide p. 445
Understand Humor	8 20	___ of 2	1 / 2	**Understand Humor:** Teacher's Guide p. 454
Vocabulary	5 16 17 15	___ of 4	3 / 4	**Vocabulary:** During independent reading time, review student's Vocabulary Journal and discuss how to improve the journal entries
Word Study Suffixes -ly, -fully	4 9	___ of 2	1 / 2	**Suffixes -ly, -fully:** Sourcebook p. 422 Teacher's Guide p. 436
Writing: Process Writing Trait: Conventions	6 11	___ of 2	1 / 2	**Trait: Conventions:** Writing Bridge 27
Form: Poem	21	___ of 1	1 / 1	**Form: Poem:** Writing Bridge 28
Writing: Grammar Conjunctions: Coordinate	2 7 13 24	___ of 4	3 / 4	**Conjunctions: Coordinate:** Writing Resource Guide p. 27 Writer's Handbook p. 29
Conjunctions: Correlative	25	___ of 1	1 / 1	**Conjunctions: Correlative:** Writing Resource Guide p. 28 Writer's Handbook p. 29
		___ / 25	18 / 25	

Answer Key

1. D   2. C   3. A   4. C   5. B   6. D   7. B   8. C   9. D   10. A   11. C   12. D   13. B

14. A   15. B   16. A   17. D   18. A   19. C   20. C   21. B   22. C   23. A   24. B   25. D

THEME 15 Ongoing Test Practice

SAMPLE
Read the passage. Then answer the question.

September 8, 2004 — I woke up this morning to the sound of the telephone ringing. When I answered it, I heard my brother's voice. He was calling to tell me that he and his wife had just had a baby.

S. Because this passage is an example of a diary, you know that —

A the writer is making up a story

B the narrator is an imaginary character

C the writer is telling about his own life

D the narrator is explaining how to do something

Read the passage. Then read each question. Circle the letter of the correct answer.

The Safety Pin Turns 157 Years Old

by Rosa Campos
Staffwriter

New York — The Museum of Inventions is excited to announce an exhibit celebrating the birthday and history of the safety pin. A man named William Hunt invented the safety pin. It was the year 1849, and Hunt was in debt. He had borrowed fifteen dollars from a friend, and he wanted to pay it back. Sadly, he did not have the money. It seemed like every penny he earned would <u>vanish</u> in a short time. What he did have, however, was talent. He had invented many useful items, such as a sewing machine, fake stone, and a stove that burned hot coal.

The man who had loaned Hunt the fifteen dollars knew that his friend had a great mind. So he decided to take a risk. He gave Hunt a piece of wire and told him to make something out of it. "I'll pay you four hundred dollars for whatever you can make with that wire," he promised. He knew that Hunt might not come up with a good idea. If that happened, the man would lose a lot of money.

Hunt took the wire and played with it. He did not have any great ideas, but he did not want to let his friend down. He also knew that if he had a good idea, he would not only be able to pay his friend back, he would also have $385 left over, which was a lot of money. The money called to him, telling him to keep trying. After twisting and turning the wire for a few hours, he noticed that it had a new shape.

The end of it was sharp like a pin. When he twisted it a little, the sharp end slid into a small pocket where it could not poke a person. With a few adjustments, Hunt created the first modern safety pin.

He took his invention to his friend, who paid him the $400. Hunt thought he had made a great deal. The friend who bought the pin used it to make a lot of money. Thousands of people wanted to buy the new pin that wouldn't poke them. That little piece of wire made him rich.

In honor of the safety pin's birthday, the Museum of Inventions is presenting an exhibit called "The History of the Safety Pin" all month long. Visitors can view the exhibit daily from 9 A.M. to 7 P.M.

1. What clue helps you figure out that this passage is an example of a news article?

   A It has a main character.
   B It has a title.
   C It tells a story.
   D It answers the questions *who, what, where, when,* and *why.*

2. Because this passage is a newspaper article, you know that —

   A the information in it is true
   B the information was made up
   C the writer wanted to express his or her feelings about safety pins
   D the writer was the person who invented the safety pin

3. What does the word <u>vanish</u> mean in this passage?

   A to save
   B to be stolen
   C to disappear
   D to get lost

4. What do you know about newspaper articles that can help you figure out that William Hunt was a real person?

   A Newspaper articles are written to entertain people.
   B Newspaper articles give facts about real events.
   C Newspaper articles tell about things that happened long ago.
   D Newspaper articles are based on stories that did not really happen.

5. Which sentence from the passage uses personification?

   A *If that happened, the man would lose a lot of money.*
   B *The friend who bought the pin used it to make a lot of money.*
   C *The money called to him, telling him to keep trying.*
   D *Visitors can view the exhibit daily from 9 A.M. to 7 P.M.*

Answer the following question on a separate sheet of paper.

6. How does knowing the genre of this passage help you understand the main idea?

THEME (15) Theme Progress Test

Read each question. Fill in the correct circle on your answer document.

1. Which of the following is an example of a compound word?

   A forest
   B underground
   C friendly
   D jumping

2. How can knowing a passage's genre help you better understand what you are reading?

   A Knowing a passage's genre helps you understand the author's opinions.
   B The genre always tells you the plot of a passage.
   C Knowing the features of a genre can help you understand the meaning of a passage.
   D Every genre involves telling a true story.

3. Which of the following sentences uses personification?

   A The setting sun told me it was time to go home.
   B The chipmunk ran up the tree when it saw the snake.
   C The door opened slowly as the dog pushed it with its nose.
   D The baby cried for her mother when she was hungry.

4. Read this passage from "Nate Murphy and the Mystery Sauropod."

   > **Day 4**
   > Everyone is up early. We're digging out the smaller bones at the top of the neck. As we uncover each new bone, we hold our breath. Will we find the skull, the rarest of dinosaur trophies?

   What does the genre of this passage help you understand about the narrator?

   A The narrator is writing a detailed report about digging for dinosaur bones.
   B The narrator is trying to write a suspenseful story about dinosaurs.
   C The narrator is writing a news article describing a day in the life of Nate Murphy.
   D The narrator is describing events in a journal as they take place.

5. Which of the following is an example of an interjection?

    A We need milk.

    B Hooray!

    C Is anyone home?

    D Go to the store.

6. Which of the following words is a compound word?

    A direction

    B lightning

    C railroad

    D wonderful

7. When you write an essay, you should always —

    A use very narrow margins

    B avoid using pictures and charts

    C put the title at the end of the essay

    D write clearly and neatly

8. What does the word <u>examine</u> mean in the sentence below?

> Mark had to <u>examine</u> the apple for a few moments to see if it was still fresh.

    A study

    B clean

    C cook

    D drop

9. Read this passage from the poem "Ancient Masters of the Earth."

> When I see the razor teeth and long tails,
> I can imagine the skeletons
> scrambling past paintings and roaring at statues.
> Do the walls tremble in fear of these beasts?

Which of these lines from the poem uses personification?

    A *When I see the razor teeth and long tails*

    B *I can imagine the skeletons*

    C *scrambling past paintings and roaring at statues*

    D *Do the walls tremble in fear of these beasts?*

10. Read this passage from "The Hatchling."

> Jonathan gently carried the egg back to the ranch in a backpack filled with hay and feathers.
>
> "I know I'm not a 'dinosaur hunter' like you, Jon," said Trevor. "But . . . the last live dinosaur hatched from an egg in Canada more than 10 years ago. And that wasn't a maiasaur."
>
> "This is a real egg, I know it!" said Jonathan. "I've been reading about maiasaurs, and the spot where we found the egg would have been perfect for a nest."

What do you know about stories that helps you better understand this passage?

A Stories are written by people called authors.

B Stories are usually based on history.

C Stories often tell about imaginary events.

D Stories have characters and a plot.

11. Which words can you combine to form a compound word?

A *pencil* and *paper*

B *book* and *desk*

C *jump* and *catch*

D *house* and *fly*

12. Which of the following visual aids should you include in a report about where dinosaurs used to live?

A a map showing places where dinosaur bones have been found

B an illustration of two dinosaurs fighting

C a chart showing what different dinosaurs liked to eat

D a photograph of an expert on dinosaurs

13. If you are writing a newspaper article about an event to make money at your school, which of the following details should you include?

A an interesting story about a past event held at your school

B what you and your classmates will be doing to make money

C how you feel about the school event

D how long you have been going to your school

Read these lines from "Ancient Masters of the Earth." Answer questions 14 and 15.

> The museum sighs with relief,
> as another day passes
> with the bones in place.
> But the halls whisper, *"Beware!"*. . .
>
> These powerless bones won't wake up.
> They are frozen in a time long, long ago.
> But millions and millions of years ago,
> these ancient masters of the Earth roamed free.

14. What clue helps you figure out that these lines are from a poem?

   A The setting is a museum at night.
   B Many of the lines are not complete sentences.
   C The lines describe the past.
   D The last word of each line ends with the same sound.

15. Which line from this passage uses personification?

   A *The museum sighs with relief*
   B *as another day passes*
   C *But millions and millions of years ago*
   D *these ancient masters of the Earth roamed free*

Choose the word that best completes each sentence for questions 16 and 17.

16. If something is _____, it is dangerous to you.

   A a method
   B a threat
   C a fossil
   D evidence

17. When you _____ someone, you know who he or she is.

   A vanish
   B scrape
   C recognize
   D method

Read this passage from "The Hatchling." Answer questions 18 and 19.

> "Oh! It's hatching!" Jenny exclaimed with delight.
>
> "Welcome to the 21st century, baby!" said Jonathan proudly as the tiny dinosaur emerged from its shell. "I think you need a name."
>
> "How about Maya?" Trevor said with a smile.

18. The genre of this passage is science fiction, so you know that —

   A a baby dinosaur egg hatched recently
   B the writer wrote about events each day as they happened
   C the events in the story did not really happen
   D the writer is telling his or her feelings about dinosaurs

19. Which line from this passage includes an interjection?

   A *"Oh! It's hatching!"*
   B *"Welcome to the 21st century, baby!"*
   C *"I think you need a name."*
   D *"How about Maya?"*

Read this passage from "Nate Murphy and the Mystery Sauropod." Answer questions 20 and 21.

> **Day 5**
>
> Today we jacket the bones so they can be moved. Jacketing is a <u>method</u> of encasing the bones in plaster-soaked burlap so they don't move or break. Someone mixes the plaster. Another cuts the burlap into big strips. A third person dips the strips in the plaster. . . . It's a lot like putting a cast on a broken leg.

20. In what way are the people in this passage alike?

   A They are all rushing to move the bones they found.
   B They are all wrapping their jackets around the bones.
   C They are all doctors who fix broken legs.
   D They all want to protect the bones they found.

21. What does the word <u>method</u> mean in this passage?

   A something that you wrap
   B something that you soak
   C a way of doing something
   D a place where bones are found

Read this passage. The sentences are numbered. Answer questions 22 and 23.

(1) Today is an exciting day for me. (2) My class is going on a field trip. (3) Before we leave, we will all have to find a partner. (4) We have to stay with our partners for the whole day. (5) This is an important rule because it helps make sure we don't get lost. (6) I wonder who my partner will be.

22. Which of the following is the best way to combine sentences 1 and 2?

   A Today is an exciting day for me, but my class is going on a field trip.
   B Today is an exciting day for me so my class is going on a field trip.
   C Today is an exciting day for me, yet my class is going on a field trip.
   D Today is an exciting day for me because my class is going on a field trip.

23. Which of the following expresses a complete thought?

   A *before we leave*
   B *we will all have to find a partner*
   C *stay with our partners for the whole day*
   D *because it helps make sure we don't get lost*

Read this passage from "T. Rex Sue Sold to Field Museum." Answer questions 24 and 25.

Chicago, Illinois—Today the Field Museum introduced Sue to the world. . . . From her small, bird-like feet to her large, sharp teeth, Sue is one big [dinosaur]! Unlike most dinosaur skeletons you see, Sue is not made of plastic or plaster.

24. Because this is a newspaper article, you can figure out that the most important information in the passage is —

   A there is a new dinosaur skeleton at the museum
   B the dinosaur skeleton comes from a Tyrannosaurus rex
   C the teeth in the dinosaur skeleton are large and sharp
   D the dinosaur skeleton's name is Sue

25. How is Sue different from most dinosaur skeletons?

   A Sue has bird-like feet.
   B Sue is very large.
   C Sue has large, sharp teeth.
   D Sue is a real dinosaur skeleton.

Student _____ Date _____

Student Theme Progress Test Record

Skills Tested	Item Numbers (cross out numbers for items answered incorrectly)	Student Score	Criterion Score	If the student scored less than the Criterion Score, use these Reteaching Tools:
Comprehension Monitor Understanding: Genre	2 4 10 14 18 24	____ of 6	5 / 6	**Monitor Understanding: Genre:** Comprehension Bridge 15
Synthesize: Classify and Categorize Information	20 25	____ of 2	1 / 2	**Synthesize: Classify and Categorize Information:** Comprehension Bridge 14
Target Skill Understand Personification	3 9 15	____ of 3	2 / 3	**Understand Personification:** Teacher's Guide p. 488
Vocabulary	8 16 17 21	____ of 4	3 / 4	**Vocabulary:** During independent reading time, review student's Vocabulary Journal and discuss how to improve the journal entries
Word Study Compound Words	1 6 11	____ of 3	2 / 3	**Compound Words:** Sourcebook p. 467 Teacher's Guide p. 486
Writing: Process Writing Trait: Presentation	7 12	____ of 2	1 / 2	**Trait: Presentation:** Writing Bridge 29
Form: Newspaper Article	13	____ of 1	1 / 1	**Form: Newspaper Article:** Writing Bridge 30
Writing: Grammar Conjunctions: Subordinate	22	____ of 1	1 / 1	**Conjunctions: Subordinate:** Writing Resource Guide p. 29 Writer's Handbook p. 29
Independent and Dependent Clauses	23	____ of 1	1 / 1	**Independent and Dependent Clauses:** Writing Resource Guide p. 30 Writer's Handbook p. 36
Interjections	5 19	____ of 2	1 / 2	**Interjections:** Writing Resource Guide p. 6 Writer's Handbook p. 29
		____ / 25	18 / 25	

Answer Key

1. B   2. C   3. A   4. D   5. B   6. C   7. D   8. A   9. D   10. C   11. D   12. A   13. B

14. B   15. A   16. B   17. C   18. C   19. A   20. D   21. C   22. D   23. B   24. A   25. D

THEME ⑯ Ongoing Test Practice

SAMPLE
Read the passage. Then answer the question.

The peanut is a very popular food in the United States. Despite its name, the peanut is not actually a nut. It is really a type of fruit called a legume. But no matter what you call it, the peanut is a delicious treat that many people enjoy eating.

S. What question helps you better understand what a peanut is?

 A What are some different brands of peanuts?
 B How is a legume different from a nut?
 C What are some other types of legumes?
 D What are some other popular foods in the United States?

Read the passage. Then read each question. Circle the letter of the correct answer.

Jorge's Discovery

Jorge was the kind of person everyone liked. He was both friendly and hard working. Many days he worked late into the night. He was trying to earn enough money to buy his own house. He saved every penny he could and bought only what he really needed.

Whenever his neighbor, Mrs. Vargas, needed something, he was there to help. He went to the store to get her groceries, and every Sunday he took her dog, Flip, down to the park to run around and play. Flip loved digging around in the dirt for buried treasures. It was on one of those Sunday trips that Jorge found something that changed his life.

He and Flip walked to the park, just like they had the <u>previous</u> Sunday. But this time there were a lot of people there. "Looks kind of crowded today, Flip," Jorge said. "Let's go for a walk by the creek instead."

Jorge took the leash off Flip so the dog could run around. While Flip played, Jorge sat on the shore and skipped rocks across the water. Then Jorge noticed Flip digging down into the dirt around a strange-looking stick. Jorge walked over and tried pulling the stick out of the ground, but it was stuck. Then he tried digging around the stick. Its <u>composition</u> was much harder than any stick he'd ever felt. Soon he realized that it wasn't a stick. It was a bone!

Jorge quickly called Flip over and put the dog's leash on. Then he ran home and called the museum to tell them he had found a very unusual bone in the park. A few hours later, he got a call from a man named Dr. Koval. He said that the bone was part of a very rare fossil.

"You made a very important find," Dr. Koval said. "That was the first claw bone of a *dryptosaurus aqualungis* ever found in this part of the country. It is very valuable. To thank you, our organization would like to give you $10,000."

Jorge couldn't believe what he was hearing! He thought the offer might be a joke, but it wasn't. A few days later, he got the money and used it to buy a nice, small house in town. But every Sunday, he still went back to see Mrs. Vargas and take Flip out for a walk.

1. What question should you ask to figure out where Jorge gets his money before the discovery?

   A Where does Jorge live?
   B What is Jorge's job?
   C Why do people like Jorge?
   D How long has Jorge been saving his money?

2. Which sentence in the beginning of the passage is an example of foreshadowing?

   A *Jorge was the kind of person everyone liked.*
   B *He was both friendly and hard working.*
   C *Whenever his neighbor, Mrs. Vargas, needed something, he was there to help.*
   D *Flip loved digging around in the dirt for buried treasures.*

3. What does the word <u>previous</u> mean in this passage?

   A always   C once
   B after   D before

4. What question might you ask to figure out why the bone Jorge found was so important?

   A What is a *dryptosaurus aqualungis*?
   B How long have Jorge and Mrs. Vargas been friends?
   C Why were there so many people at the park that Sunday?
   D What is Dr. Koval's first name?

5. What does the word <u>composition</u> mean in this passage?

   A what something is made of
   B the weight of an object
   C the shape of an object
   D what something looks like

Answer the following question on a separate sheet of paper.

6. Based on the passage, what kind of organization does Dr. Koval probably work for?

THEME 16 Theme Progress Test

Read each question. Fill in the correct circle on your answer document.

1. When an author gives you hints about something that will happen later in a story, it is called —

   A genre
   B personification
   C flashback
   D foreshadowing

2. What is the past tense form of the verb <u>draw</u>?

   A drawed   C drew
   B drawded   D drewed

3. Which word best completes the chart below?

laugh	dance	clap
laughing	dancing	?

   A claping
   B clapping
   C claped
   D clapped

4. Asking questions before you start reading will help you —

   A summarize what you read
   B determine the author's reason for writing
   C make predictions about the text
   D connect new ideas and information

5. Which word best completes the sentence below?

   The boat filled with water and then _____ to the bottom of the lake.

   A sink
   B sinked
   C sanked
   D sank

6. Read this passage from "The Case of the Missing Capsule."

> We cheered. We had found the capsule, but the items were still a mystery. Inside we found an ad for a new color TV. There was also a picture of Elvis Presley.

What might you ask to help you better understand when the items were put in the capsule?

A When did Elvis Presley live?

B Why were the items a mystery?

C Where did they find the capsule?

D When did they find the capsule?

7. For which of the following words should you double the consonant when adding the suffix *-ed*?

A look

B brag

C care

D wash

8. Read this passage from "Saving Mammoth Cave."

> I arrived at Army headquarters to register for the CCC. I was assigned to Mammoth Cave in Kentucky. As soon as I stepped on the bus, I noticed it was full of men about my age, 19. Everyone looked as nervous as I did!

Which of the following questions should you ask to help you better understand this passage?

A Did any of the speaker's friends join the CCC?

B How many people were on the bus with the speaker?

C What time of day did the speaker arrive at Army headquarters?

D What was the speaker going to do at Mammoth Cave?

9. Which word best completes the chart below?

look	practice	write
looked	practiced	?

A wrote

B writed

C wroted

D writted

10. What does the word <u>significant</u> mean in the sentence below?

> My graduation from high school was one of the most <u>significant</u> events of my life.

A easy to forget
B important
C fun to talk about
D boring

11. Read this passage from "Race Against Time: David Sucec Records Ancient Art."

> To protect the art, we cannot touch it. The oils in our skin affect the art. In less than 15 minutes, one person can do more damage to a rock art panel than thousands of years of erosion. We need to respect this art from ancient people.

Which question should you ask to help you better understand this passage?

A What kind of paint did ancient people use?
B How much is the art worth?
C How do the oils in our skin damage the art?
D How big are the paintings?

Read this passage. The passage contains errors. Answer questions 12 and 13.

> (1) It was snowing vary hard outside? (2) Adam and Phil spent the whole day at the park. (3) Building a snowman with the snow, branches, and materials they found around them. (4) When they finished their snowman, they called their friends over to see it.

12. What is the best way to rewrite sentence 1?

A It was snowing very hard outside.
B it was snowing very hard outside!
C It was snowing vary hard outside!
D It was snowing vary hard outside.

13. Which sentence from the passage is a fragment?

A sentence 1
B sentence 2
C sentence 3
D sentence 4

Read this passage from "The Case of the Missing Capsule." Answer questions 14 and 15.

> We all breathed a sigh of relief as Mrs. Napoli held up an envelope. On it written in bold, black letters were the words . . . ***Fourth Graders of 2008.*** Mrs. Napoli said, "This letter has been kept for us in the library for the past 50 years."
>
> *May 1, 1958*
> *Dear Fourth Graders of 2008,*
> *Hello from fifty years ago! We have buried a time capsule with items from 1958.*

14. The letter in this passage is an example of —

   A metaphor   **C** symbolism
   B flashback   **D** foreshadowing

15. Because this passage comes from a story, you know that —

   A the events in the passage happened a short time ago
   B the passage will give facts about someone's life
   C the people in the passage are made up
   D the passage contains only facts

Read this passage from "Saving Mammoth Cave." Answer questions 16 and 17.

> **December 9, 1935**
> What an exciting day! While we were working on the trails, our park guides found the remains of someone who lived long ago. We helped move a boulder off the trapped remains so scientists can study the find.

16. Which question should you ask to help you better understand why the speaker was in the park?

   A What kind of rock was the boulder made of?
   B How many scientists will study the remains?
   C Which trail was the speaker working on?
   D What kind of work was the speaker doing when the remains were found?

17. This passage comes from a diary, which means that —

   A this is the way the writer remembers the events of the day
   B this story was published in a newspaper in December
   C the writer made the story up so people would laugh
   D the writer wants to teach the reader about caves

Choose the word that best completes each sentence for questions 18 and 19.

18. A huge sheet of slow-moving ice is called _____.

    A a survey

    B erosion

    C a glacier

    D splendor

19. When wind, rain, snow, and other conditions cause the land to break into small pieces and move around, it is called _____.

    A composition

    B splendor

    C survey

    D erosion

Read these sentences from "Swept Away." Answer questions 20 and 21.

> Fast-moving storms can sweep away roads, beaches, and neighborhoods. . . .
>
> September 1998 — For years, the coastal beauty of Bay St. Louis, Mississippi, attracted many visitors.
>
> August 2005 — Hurricane Katrina changed Bay St. Louis forever. Powerful winds destroyed houses and even ripped the leaves off the trees!

20. To better understand about fast-moving storms, you should ask —

    A how hurricanes get their names

    B how long Hurricane Katrina lasted

    C how Bay St. Louis got its name

    D how many people visit Bay St. Louis each year

21. Which information would you add to the passage to explain how Bay St. Louis has changed since 1998?

    A the number of houses that need to be rebuilt

    B how hard Hurricane Katrina's winds blew

    C the kinds of trees that grow in Bay St. Louis

    D whether or not scientists predict future storms

> [She said,] "There was a hurricane in 1960 that slammed our area. Look at this article."
>
> *Because of the swelling floodwaters from Hurricane Donna, crews built a makeshift dam out of stone and rock behind South Shore Elementary School. Luckily, the dam helped <u>prevent</u> the water from flooding the town square.*
>
> "School Creek must have flooded, and the water probably washed away the soil and the time capsule," Jake said. "Now we'll never know where the capsule went!"
>
> "Look at the picture," Latanya said. It showed our very own creek filled up with water, and at the end of it was a small stone dam.

22. Which paragraph in this passage is an example of a flashback?

   A the first paragraph   **C** the third paragraph

   B the second paragraph   **D** the last paragraph

23. What does the word <u>prevent</u> mean in this passage?

   A soak   **C** stop

   B flood   **D** move

Read this passage. The sentences contain errors. Answer questions 24 and 25.

> (1) Traya stood outside the door while she waded for Steve. (2) Steve came running down the stares and rushed out the door. (3) He was going so fast that he almost missed his friend.

24. What change should you make to sentence 1?

   A change <u>stood</u> to <u>standed</u>

   B change <u>Steve</u> to <u>steve</u>

   C change <u>while</u> to <u>because</u>

   D change <u>waded</u> to <u>waited</u>

25. What change should you make in sentence 2?

   A change <u>stares</u> to <u>stairs</u>

   B change the period to a question mark

   C change <u>rushed</u> to <u>rushes</u>

   D change <u>running</u> to <u>runing</u>

THEME 16

Student Theme Progress Test Record

Skills Tested	Item Numbers (cross out numbers for items answered incorrectly)	Student Score	Criterion Score	If the student scored less than the Criterion Score, use these Reteaching Tools:
Comprehension Ask Questions: Meaning	4 6 8 11 16 20	_____ of 6	5 / 6	**Ask Questions: Meaning:** Comprehension Bridge 16
Monitor Understanding: Genre	15 17	_____ of 2	1 / 2	**Monitor Understanding: Genre:** Comprehension Bridge 15
Target Skill Identify Foreshadowing and Flashback	1 14 22	_____ of 3	2 / 3	**Identify Foreshadowing and Flashback:** Teacher's Guide p. 511
Vocabulary	10 18 19 23	_____ of 4	3 / 4	**Vocabulary:** During independent reading time. review student's Vocabulary Journal and discuss how to improve the journal entries
Word Study Consonant Doubling	3 7	_____ of 2	1 / 2	**Consonant Doubling:** Sourcebook p. 484 Teacher's Guide p. 502
Writing: Process Writing Process: Editing	12 13	_____ of 2	1 / 2	**Process: Editing:** Writing Bridge 31
Organizational Pattern: Compare and Contrast	21	_____ of 1	1 / 1	**Organizational Pattern: Compare and Contrast:** Writing Bridge 32
Writing: Grammar Homophones	24 25	_____ of 2	1 / 2	**Homophones:** Writing Resource Guide p. 32 Writer's Handbook p. 31
Irregular Verbs	2 5 9	_____ of 3	2 / 3	**Irregular Verbs:** Writing Resource Guide p. 16 Writer's Handbook p. 25
		_____ / 25	17 / 25	

Answer Key

1. D   2. C   3. B   4. C   5. D   6. A   7. B   8. D   9. A   10. B   11. C   12. A   13. C

14. B   15. C   16. D   17. A   18. C   19. D   20. B   21. A   22. B   23. C   24. D   25. A

End-of-Year Review

Read the passage. Then read each question. Fill in the circle on your answer document.

Carlo and Mrs. Steel

Carlo and his friend Gil were out in his backyard one afternoon playing baseball with some other kids in the neighborhood. They enjoyed getting together each week to play. It was the last inning, and Carlo's team was behind by two runs. It was Carlo's turn to bat, and he knew that if he hit a home run his team would win the game.

He stepped up to home plate and gripped the bat tightly. He leaned over and held it over his shoulder, ready to swing when the moment was right. Even though there was a lot of pressure on him, Carlo knew that he could knock the ball out of the yard.

The pitcher threw the ball and Carlo swung. There was a loud "CRACK!" as the bat connected with the ball. Everybody cheered as they watched the ball sail high into the air and out over the fence. Suddenly the kids heard something else. It was the crash of breaking glass.

Carlo's excitement at hitting a home run quickly changed to fear. He knew exactly what had happened. The ball he hit had broken something. The game stopped as everybody ran over to the fence to see where the ball went.

"Uh-oh," said Gil. "It was Mrs. Steel's house. You're up to your neck in trouble now!"

Those words hit Carlo like a hammer hitting a nail. All of the kids in town talked about Mrs. Steel. They <u>claimed</u> she was the meanest person they had ever known. The funny thing was that Carlo had never met anyone who actually knew her. Everyone just talked about her.

Carlo's mother had been working inside when she heard the crash. When she came out, the kids explained what had happened. She sent them all home and walked over to Mrs. Steel's house with Carlo. She made him explain to Mrs. Steel what had happened and offer to pay for the window out of his allowance.

"Oh, I don't think that's necessary," Mrs. Steel said. Carlo could not believe what he was hearing. Was Mrs. Steel sticking up for him? Then she said, "I'll tell you what. I have a lot of work for a young boy to do around here. If Carlo comes by every Saturday for a month to help me with some chores, I'll pay for the window."

"That sounds fair," Carlo's mother replied. "I'm sure he would be happy to help out."

"Rats!" Carlo thought to himself. "I bet she was just pretending to be nice so that she could be mean to me for a whole month."

That Saturday Carlo went over to Mrs. Steel's house. He was sure that he was going to have an awful day. He knocked on the door and she invited him in. She showed him around the house and explained that the first thing he would do is wash all of the windows. She gave him some glass cleaner and paper towels.

"You can listen to the radio while you work if you like," she said. "Go ahead and turn on any station you want."

"Thanks," Carlo said as he fiddled with the radio knobs for a moment. Soon the sounds of rock music filled the house. He found himself dancing as he made his way from window to window. A little later, Mrs. Steel brought him some lemonade and carrot sticks for a snack. He took a break and they sat and talked.

"You know, I don't get many visitors. It's nice to have someone to talk to," Mrs. Steel said. "And you're such a nice boy to help me out like this."

"Well, I did break your window," Carlo said. "It's only fair that I make it up to you. Besides, I'm actually having fun. You're a really nice lady, Mrs. Steel. I'm glad I can help you."

After his snack, Carlo went back to work. He finished his chores for the day and then went home. For the next three weeks, he went back to Mrs. Steel's house every Saturday to mow her lawn, take out her trash, and do whatever else she needed.

After he finished his work on the last Saturday, he got ready to leave and said, "OK, I'll see you next week, Mrs. Steel."

"But Carlo," she said, "This was your last week. You don't have to come back anymore."

"I want to come back," Carlo responded with a smile. "I've really enjoyed spending time with you. Is it OK for me to come over again next week?"

"That would be nice," she answered with a smile. "See you next Saturday."

1. Which information in the first paragraph is most important?

   A The kids enjoyed playing baseball.
   B It was up to Carlo to win the game.
   C The kids were in Carlo's backyard.
   D They were playing in the afternoon.

2. Which of the following words is an antonym of <u>tightly</u>?

   A strongly
   B incorrectly
   C loosely
   D happily

3. Carlo probably changed his mind about Mrs. Steel because —

A she was nice to him whenever he came over

B his mother told him that Mrs. Steel was very nice

C she told him it was OK to keep coming over to visit

D his friends thought that Mrs. Steel was the nicest lady in town

4. Who is the main character in this story?

A Carlo

B Mrs. Steel

C Carlo's mother

D Gil

5. What does the word <u>claimed</u> mean in this story?

A to be curious about something

B to be afraid of somebody

C to say that something is true

D to believe that something is true

6. What do Carlo and Gil have in common?

A Both broke Mrs. Steel's window.

B Both think Mrs. Steel is a nice lady.

C Both like to clean windows.

D Both enjoy playing baseball.

7. Which of these sentences from the story contains an opinion?

A *That Saturday Carlo went over to Mrs. Steel's house.*

B *The ball he hit had broken something.*

C *"You're a really nice lady, Mrs. Steel."*

D *He finished his chores for the day and then went home.*

8. Which of the following questions would help you better understand the meaning of this story?

A Why did people think Mrs. Steel was mean?

B Who won the baseball game?

C How much did it cost to fix the window?

D Did the kids get together for another baseball game?

9. Read this line from the story.

> "You're up to your neck in trouble now!"

What does the phrase up to your neck in trouble mean?

A You are no longer in trouble.

B You have a big problem.

C Nothing is wrong that you can't fix.

D You have a pain in your neck.

10. In the beginning of this story, you learn —

A how the main problem in the story is solved

B how the characters feel about the solution to the problem

C what the main problem in the story is

D what the characters will do to solve the problem

Read the passage. Then read each question. Fill in the circle on your answer document.

Paul Revere

Paul Revere was born in Boston on January 1, 1734. At the time, Massachusetts was still a colony. The United States had not been formed yet. The people in America were ruled by the king of England.

As a young boy, Paul attended the North Writing School. He stayed there for only a short time. Then, like many boys his age, he became an apprentice. He went to work for a silversmith who taught him how to make beautiful forks, spoons, pots, and other things out of silver.

When Paul was a young man, he went off to fight in a war for a year. When he got back, he got married and opened up his own silver shop. He worked mostly with silver and gold, but he also decided to try some other things. He became very good at copper <u>plate</u> engraving. These plates were used to make pictures for books, magazines, and business cards. He also worked as a dentist for a few years, cleaning people's teeth and putting together false teeth made of animal teeth or wire and ivory.

Like many people at that time, Paul held the <u>belief</u> that people in America should be free to make their own government. He did not think it was fair that they were ruled by a country on the other side of the ocean. People who felt this way were called patriots.

The most famous event of Paul's life happened in 1775. He was working as an express rider. This meant that he took news, messages, and important documents and delivered them to places far away. There were no cars, trains, or airplanes at the time, so he had to ride a horse. On the night of April 17, 1775, two men hung lanterns in the Old North Church in Boston. This was a secret signal. It meant that British soldiers were coming across the river in a boat. They were planning on arresting the patriots. Paul's job was to warn everyone that the soldiers were on their way.

Paul set out on horseback to warn everyone. Paul decided that he was going to make as much noise as he could so that everyone would know what was happening. As he rode, he shouted, "The regulars are out!" The regulars were the British soldiers. Everyone knew what the message meant. They gathered together and went to protect Boston.

Many people think that Paul Revere was the only person who went out that night to warn people. There were actually three other men who also made the predawn ride. William Dawes went out at the same time as Paul Revere, headed in a different direction. A man named Dr. Samuel Prescott was returning home late that night when he heard the warning. He decided to join in and help spread the word. A fourth man, Israel Bissell, also went out to warn people. In fact, he made the longest ourney, traveling all the way from Massachusetts to Pennsylvania. Thanks to him, people all over the Northeast were warned that the British soldiers were getting ready to attack.

Paul Revere is not thought of as the most important rider because of what he did that night. He is remembered because of a famous poem about what happened that night, called "Paul Revere's Ride," written by a man named Henry Wadsworth Longfellow. The opening lines of the poem read:

> *Listen, my children, and you shall hear*
> *Of the midnight ride of Paul Revere*
> *On the eighteenth of April in Seventy-Five*
> *Hardly a man is now alive*
> *Who remembers that famous day and year.*

Over the next few years, life in America changed a great deal. The United States of America was formed and the Revolutionary War was fought. Paul helped the United States win the war, and then he went back to Boston. He died many years later in 1818, but he continues to be remembered as an important patriot who helped bring freedom to America.

11. Which of these sentences from the passage tells you about the job Paul Revere is best remembered for?

   A *Paul helped the United States win the war, and then he went back to Boston.*
   B *When he got back, he got married and opened up his own silver shop.*
   C *As a young boy, Paul attended the North Writing School.*
   D *Paul set out on horseback to warn everyone.*

12. In what way has sending messages over long distances changed since 1775?

   A Messages are sent much faster now.
   B Messages are sent much slower now.
   C Messages are sent only in writing now.
   D Messages cannot be sent over long distances now.

13. What connection can you make between the patriots in 1775 and people living in America today?

   A Both live in colonies.
   B Both are ruled by the king of England.
   C Both believe people should be free.
   D Both only go to school for only a short time when they are children.

14. What feature does the poem in this passage include?

   A repetition of language
   B rhyming words
   C an analogy
   D foreshadowing

15. Read the meanings below for the word plate.

> **plate**
>
> **1.** something you eat food off of
> **2.** a metal tag on a car **3.** a base in baseball **4.** a surface from which to print

Which meaning best fits the way plate is used in the passage?

A meaning 1
B meaning 2
C meaning 3
D meaning 4

16. *Pilot* is to *airplane* as *express rider* is to —

A *lantern*
B *horse*
C *message*
D *swift*

17. What question would you ask based on the information in paragraph 2 of the passage?

A Why did boys at that time become apprentices?
B Who was the teacher at the North Writing School?
C Was there also a South Writing School?
D What is the difference between silver and gold?

18. Read this sentence from the passage.

> There were actually three other men who also made the predawn ride.

The prefix *pre-* in the word predawn shows that —

A the men rode after dawn
B the men rode before dawn
C the men rode at dawn
D the men rode again at dawn

19. What do you know about Henry Wadsworth Longfellow's poem "Paul Revere's Ride"?

A The information in the poem is all true
B The events in the poem took place recently.
C Longfellow was trying to express his feelings about Paul Revere in the poem.
D Longfellow rode with Paul Revere on the famous night.

20. As used in this passage, the word belief means something a person —

A does for fun
B cannot remember
C does not like
D thinks is true

Read the passage. Then read each question. Fill in the circle on your answer document.

The Ice Cream Maker

Just like every other year on the Fourth of July, we went to visit my grandparents. They have a big farm out in the country. My aunt, uncle, and cousins came over for a big picnic. My father and Uncle Jim were cooking hamburgers and hot dogs on the grill. My mother and Aunt Lucy were helping Grandma prepare salads in the kitchen. Some of my cousins were throwing a flying disc around, and my brothers were swimming down at the pond.

I was sitting on the back steps watching everyone. Grandpa walked over and sat down beside me. "Having fun, Timmy?" he asked.

"Yep!" I responded. "I was playing with the other kids, but then I got hot so I decided to sit in the shade. What are you doing?"

"Oh, I was helping out in the kitchen, and then I decided to check on your father," Grandpa explained. "He's doing a good job on those burgers and dogs. I think we'll be ready to eat pretty soon. Are you looking forward to the fireworks tonight?"

"I'm looking forward to the ice cream!" I said with a big smile. Most of the time when my family had ice cream, we bought it at a store. But when we came up for the Independence Day picnic at Grandma and Grandpa's house, we always had fresh, homemade ice cream.

"Oh, you are, are you?" Grandpa said with a grin. "Are you going to help make it this year?"

"You know I always help!" I answered, laughing. Making ice cream with the old ice cream machine was a lot of hard work. First we had to drag the big metal tub out of the barn. Then Grandpa would put some blocks of ice in it and cover them with a special blanket. After that the kids would hit the blanket with hammers to break the ice into tiny pieces.

While we got the ice ready, Grandma would be in the kitchen making the ice cream mixture. She would stir up milk, cream, fruit, and sugar to make a sweet blend that would turn into ice cream. When it was ready, she would pour it into the ice cream maker.

Once the ice was broken into small pieces, Grandpa would put the ice cream maker into the tub. Then the older kids would take turns turning the crank. You had to keep the ice cream mix moving around or else it would not freeze right. Turning the crank is hard work, so people take turns. The younger kids would take turns sitting on top of the ice cream maker to keep it from moving around too much. Every few minutes, Grandpa would pour rock salt on the ice. This helped it to melt faster. The faster the ice in the tub melted, the faster the ice cream in the machine froze. Making ice cream is a job that takes the whole family to complete!

"You know, I think you might be old enough to take a turn on the crank this year," Grandpa said with a <u>thoughtful</u> look. "Think you're up to the job?"

My heart started pounding. It was the most important job of all. "I'm ready," I told him. "I'll be the best cranker you ever saw!"

A few minutes later, lunch was served and we all sat down to eat. The food was <u>plentiful</u>, and everybody talked and told stories while they ate, except for me. I spent the whole time thinking about making the ice cream. I hoped I would do a good job.

A few hours later, Grandpa announced that it was time to make the ice cream. I watched as the older kids and Grandpa got everything ready outside.

My cousin Toby took the first turn running the crank. He was a few years older than me and had made ice cream with Grandpa many times. When his turn was over, Grandpa looked at me and said, "OK, Timmy, you're up!"

I wrapped my fingers around the crank and started to turn it. At first I couldn't get the handle to move. Then I pushed really hard and it started to go. I turned the crank again and again. The longer I worked it, the easier it became. Before long Grandpa put his hand on my shoulder and said, "OK, let me check it."

He opened the container and smiled, saying, "Wow, it's already done! Great work, Timmy!"

I had a <u>massive</u> smile on my face as he scooped out the ice cream into cones for everyone to eat. Some people gobbled it down quickly that night, but not me. I took my time and ate it slowly as we watched the fireworks. I was as happy as a clam. It was the best ice cream I'd ever had.

21. Which sentence best summarizes the first paragraph?

   A The speaker's cousins were playing football.

   B The speaker was helping the family prepare the meal.

   C Everyone in the speaker's family was busy doing something.

   D The speaker's aunt and uncle are named Lucy and Jim.

22. If you wanted to write a story similar to this one, what would be the best way to organize it?

   A strongest argument to weakest argument

   B the first event to the last event

   C most important information to least important information

   D least important information to most important information

23. What does the word <u>plentiful</u> mean in this story?

A something with a bad taste
B something with a pleasing taste
C not enough of something
D more than enough of something

24. Read this part of the story.

> My heart started pounding. It was the most important job of all. "I'm ready," I told him. "I'll be the best cranker you ever saw!"

Which of the following best describes how the writer feels in this passage?

A excited
B scared
C bored
D relaxed

25. Where does this story take place?

A in a meadow
B on an island
C in a big city
D on a farm

26. Why is Timmy's family having a picnic in this story?

A They have a lot of extra food to get rid of.
B They are having a party for Timmy's birthday.
C They are celebrating Independence Day.
D They want to see how well their new grill works.

27. You can tell from the information in the passage that the word <u>massive</u> means —

A large
B angry
C small
D unhappy

28. Which of these sentences from the story contains a simile?

A *I hoped I would do a good job.*
B *I was as happy as a clam.*
C *Grandpa walked over and sat down beside me.*
D *Making ice cream with the old ice cream machine was a lot of hard work.*

29. What does the word <u>thoughtful</u> mean?

A with a lot of thought
B without thought
C before thinking
D after thinking

30. How do you know this story is realistic?

A The narrator and his family had a picnic on the Fourth of July.
B The narrator enjoyed making ice cream.
C The events in this story happened a long time ago.
D The events in this story could really take place.

Read the passage. Then read each question. Fill in the circle on your answer document.

The Amazing Pencil

Did you ever stop to take a close look at a pencil? Nearly all pencils are made mostly of wood. At one end they have a metal piece with a small pink eraser, while the other end is flat. In the center is a hard, dark graphite stick. When you sharpen the flat end, it turns into a point you can write with.

The very first kind of pencil was invented in <u>ancient</u> Rome. It wasn't made of wood or used to write on paper. It was a thin metal stick made of lead. It was called a stylus, and people used it to write on a kind of paper called papyrus.

People began using <u>graphite</u> for writing sometime in the early 1500s. At the time, a large amount of this kind of rock was found in England. It could be cut up into sticks. While the sticks were good for writing, they were very soft, so they broke quickly. To make sure this did not happen, the writer would first wrap string or sheep skin around a stick.

News about the new writing tool spread all over the world. These early pencils were so rare that often only very wealthy people owned them. The pencil was in high demand because it was much cleaner and easier to use than ink. Years later, a couple from Italy got the idea to put the graphite into wood. They took a piece of juniper wood and hollowed it out. Then they put the graphite inside. They soon invented an even better method. Instead of drilling a hole in a piece of wood, they made two pencil halves and put the graphite between them. Then they glued the halves together. This is the same method that is usually used today.

Even though it became easier to make pencils over time, it became harder to find good graphite to put in them. Most graphite crumbled when you tried to cut it. Then during the Napoleonic Wars, a scientist in France had an idea. He took some small pieces of graphite and mixed them with clay. Then he molded the mixture into sticks and cooked them in a special oven called a kiln. When the sticks were done, they were hard enough to write with. Word spread about this discovery, and soon everybody was making their pencils this way.

In 1858 a man named Hyman Lipman improved the pencil again. He was tired of having to reach for an eraser every time he made a mistake. So one day he cut a small chunk off of a big eraser and attached it to the end of his pencil with a piece of metal. It worked like a charm. Before long, pencils were being made with erasers already attached.

Today pencils are no longer made by hand. Large machines cut the wood into small sticks. Special devices grind up graphite and clay into powder. Then they mix the powder with water and roll it into long strings like spaghetti. These strings are heated in a kiln and then cut into pencil-sized pieces. These pieces are put between wo pieces of wood, which are then glued together. Next the wood sticks are painted or coated with a clear paint called <u>varnish</u>. In the United States, pencils are usually yellow. Pencils made in Germany are often green, while pencils manufactured in Switzerland are usually red. In the United Kingdom, pencils are yellow with a black stripe. In India, they are red with a black stripe.

If you read the writing on a pencil, you will see that the pencil has a number. Most of the pencils students use to write with are number two pencils. What does that mean? The number tells you how hard the graphite is—the lower the number, the softer the graphite. Number two is the best hardness for writing. Harder pencils are used by artists. They use different numbers to make darker or lighter lines when they draw.

There are many different types of pencils used today. Carpenters use a flat type of pencil that won't roll. The piece of graphite is much bigger, which is ideal for drawing on boards. Many people in the business world use mechanical pencils. These are pencils made of plastic or metal. To use them, you put a small, thin piece of graphite inside and click the top or twist the whole pencil. Whenever you need more graphite, you just click or twist the pencil again.

No matter what they look like or how they are made, pencils have made life easier for people all over the world.

31. According to the information in this passage, why did people put the graphite into wooden sticks?

   A The graphite broke easily when there was nothing to protect it.
   B People wanted their pencils to be more colorful.
   C The graphite would not leave a mark on the paper unless it was in a wooden stick.
   D People wanted their pencils to look more like pens.

32. In the 1500s a pencil was often considered a symbol of a person's —

   A age
   B wealth
   C strength
   D popularity

33. By reading on in the passage, you can figure out that <u>graphite</u> is —

A a type of wood used to make pencils

B a type of lead used long ago by people who lived in Rome

C a kind of rock that leaves a mark when you rub it on paper

D the piece of metal that holds an eraser on the end of a pencil

34. As used in this passage, the word <u>ancient</u> means —

A from long ago

B from far away

C from another country

D from nearby

35. Which sentence from the passage describes a type of pencil?

A *Today pencils are no longer made by hand.*

B *Then they put the graphite inside.*

C *He took some small pieces of graphite and mixed them with clay.*

D *Carpenters use a flat type of pencil that won't roll.*

36. Which of these sentences from the passage is an opinion?

A *Special devices grind up graphite and clay into powder.*

B *It wasn't made of wood or used to write on paper.*

C *Number two is the best hardness for writing.*

D *These are pencils made of plastic or metal.*

37. To understand what a stylus is, what question should you ask?

A Who invented the stylus?

B What kind of mark did the stylus leave on the papyrus?

C How is papyrus different from modern paper?

D What else did the Romans invent?

38. In what way are the couple from Italy and Hyman Lipman alike?

A They both changed the way pencils are made.

B They both put erasers on pencils.

C They both used flat pencils that would not roll.

D They both used papyrus.

39. Which of these sentences from the passage includes a simile?

A *Nearly all pencils are made mostly of wood.*

B *Harder pencils are used by artists.*

C *In India, they are red with a black stripe.*

D *It worked like a charm.*

40. Which words from the passage help you figure out the meaning of the word <u>varnish</u>?

A *graphite* and *clay*

B *wood* and *glued*

C *clear* and *paint*

D *heated* and *kiln*

Read the passage. Then read each question. Fill in the circle on your answer document.

Roddy the Rooster

"Not again!" Peaches the pig groaned and complained as she heard the rooster crow out in the barnyard. "Every morning it's the same thing. Here I am trying to get some rest and that bird starts screaming at the top of his lungs. How is a lady supposed to get her beauty sleep with that all that racket going on?"

She marched out into the pigpen and waited for the farmer to bring breakfast. Peaches loved her breakfast and didn't know what she would do without it. The farmer arrived a few minutes later and poured a <u>layer</u> of food along the inside of the long trough. As the pigs gathered around to eat, Peaches got an idea.

"Whenever I get a sore throat, it hurts too much to talk," she said to herself. "I bet that if that rooster had a sore throat, he wouldn't be able to crow and wake me up. I would finally be able to get some sleep!"

Later that day, the sneaky pig walked over to talk to the rooster. "Hi, Roddy. How are you doing?" she asked, wearing her sweetest smile. "You know, I've heard that roosters can only crow loudly in the morning," Peaches said. "Is that true?"

"Of course not," he answered. "I can crow that loud at any time, day or night."

"I don't believe you," Peaches responded. "Let's hear you try to crow right now. <u>Impress</u> me."

With that, Roddy let out the same ear-splitting crow that Peaches had heard early that morning, but she pretended not to hear it. "Is that the best you can do?" she asked. "Why, if I didn't see your beak move, I would have sworn that you didn't make a sound."

Roddy let out another crow, even louder than the one before. Once again Peaches acted like she could barely hear him. Again and again Roddy let out deafening crows that could be heard all over the countryside. Finally he had to stop.

"I'm sorry," Roddy said. "I think I'm getting a sore throat from all that crowing."

"That's OK," Peaches replied. "We can try again tomorrow."

The next morning Peaches woke up and smiled. It was peaceful and quiet. All the other pigs were still sleeping. "I guess I'll have breakfast all to myself," she said as she went out into the pigpen. "It's probably been sitting there for hours."

But when she got outside there was no breakfast. She waited and waited, but the farmer never came. He was still fast asleep inside the farmhouse! Peaches looked around the barnyard and realized that everyone was still sleeping except for her and poor Roddy, who was too sick to crow.

As she sat in the dirt with her stomach growling, Peaches began to realize how valuable Roddy's crowing was. If he didn't wake everyone up, nothing on the farm would get done on time. After the farmer finally came out and got the day started, Peaches went over to take care of Roddy. She helped him get over his sore throat, and the next morning he was as good as new.

41. Which of these sentences from the passage uses personification?

   A *If he didn't wake everyone up, nothing on the farm could get done on time.*
   B *He was still fast asleep inside the farmhouse!*
   C *Roddy let out another crow, even louder than the one before.*
   D *Later that day, the sneaky pig walked over to talk to the rooster.*

42. In what way are the other pigs similar to the farmer?

   A They sleep in the farmhouse.
   B They eat in the pigpen.
   C They rely on the rooster to wake them up.
   D They think Roddy crows too loudly.

43. As used in this passage, what does the word <u>impress</u> mean?

   A amaze
   B bore
   C ask
   D upset

44. Early in the story, Peaches says that she doesn't know what she would do without her breakfast. This is an example of —

   A flashback   C metaphor
   B foreshadowing   D simile

45. Where is the resolution to this story?

   A in the first paragraph
   B in paragraph 3
   C in paragraph 7
   D in the last paragraph

46. How does Peaches try to solve her problem in this passage?

   A She explains her problem to the rooster and asks him for help.
   B She covers her ears so she can't hear the rooster crow in the morning.
   C She tells the rooster that the farmer is mad at him for crowing so loudly.
   D She makes the rooster crow until he gets a sore throat.

47. Which words from the first paragraph help you understand how Peaches felt?

   A *groaned* and *complained*
   B *rooster* and *crow*
   C *barnyard* and *morning*
   D *beauty* and *sleep*

48. What does Peaches have in common with Grandpa in the story "The Ice Cream Maker"?

   A They both like to make ice cream.
   B They both live on a farm.
   C They both dislike roosters.
   D They both like to sleep late.

49. What does the word <u>layer</u> mean in this passage?

   A large amount   C long, flat pile
   B small amount   D short, high pile

50. How can you tell that this story is fiction?

   A The author expresses his opinions.
   B Animals don't really talk.
   C The events in this story really happened.
   D Roosters don't really live on farms.

End-of-Year Review

Extended Response Questions

1. Read the passage "The Amazing pencil." How have pencils changed since the 1500s?

2. Read the passage "Paul Revere." Why were British soldiers planning to arrest the patriots?

....

End-of-Year Review

Writing Prompt

Most people have had at least one really great day that they will always remember.

Think about a time that you had a really great day.

Now write a story about your really great day.

Hints for responding to the writing prompt:
- Read the prompt carefully.
- Use prewriting strategies to organize your ideas.
- Include details that help explain your main idea.
- Write sentences in different ways.
- Use words that mean exactly what you want to say.
- Look over your essay when you are done and correct any mistakes.

End-of-Year Review Test Record

Comprehension

Cross out numbers for items answered incorrectly.

Make Connections	13	Make Connections: Text to Text, Self, and World	12 48
Determine Importance	1	Determine Importance: Purpose for Reading	11 35
Infer	3	Infer: Fact/Opinion	7 36
Create Images	24	Create Images: Enhance Understanding	47
Use Fix-Up Strategies	40	Use Fix-Up Strategies: Read On	27 33
Synthesize	21	Synthesize: Classify/Categorize Information	6 42
Monitor Understanding	26	Monitor Understanding: Genre	19 30 50
Ask Questions	17	Ask Questions: Meaning	8 37

If student has difficulty with comprehension, use the Comprehension Bridges.

Total Comprehension Score ____ / 24

Target Skills

Identify Story Structure	10	Identify Character	4
Identify Plot	45	Understand Simile	28 39
Identify Setting	25	Recognize Rhythm and Rhyme	14
Identify Analogies	16	Understand Personification	41
Understand Symbolism	32	Identify Foreshadowing and Flashback	44

If student has difficulty with Target Skills, use the Teacher's Guide lessons.

Total Target Skills Score ____ / 11

Vocabulary

If student has difficulty with vocabulary, review student's Vocabulary Journal.

5 20 23 34 43 49

Total Vocabulary Score ____ / 6

Word Study

Synonyms and Antonyms	2	Idioms	9
Multiple-Meaning Words	15	Suffixes *-ful, -able, -less*	29
Prefixes *re-, pre-*	18		

If student has difficulty with Word Study, use Sourcebook and Teacher's Guide lessons.

Total Word Study Score ____ / 5

Writing: Process Writing

Organizational Pattern: Sequential	22	Organizational Pattern: Cause and Effect	31
Organizational Pattern: Problem and Solution	46	Organizational Pattern: Compare/Contrast	38

If student has difficulty with Process Writing, use Writing Bridges.

Total Writing: Process Writing Score ____ / 4

Total Score ____ / 50

Answer Key

1. B	6. D	11. D	16. B	21. C	26. C	31. A	36. C	41. D	46. D
2. C	7. C	12. A	17. A	22. B	27. A	32. B	37. B	42. C	47. A
3. A	8. A	13. C	18. B	23. D	28. B	33. C	38. A	43. A	48. B
4. A	9. B	14. B	19. C	24. A	29. A	34. A	39. D	44. B	49. C
5. C	10. C	15. D	20. D	25. D	30. D	35. D	40. C	45. D	50. B

Extended Response Questions

1. What are some ways that the Kahlos and the Batalis are connected in "The Mystery of the Box in the Wall"?

2. What connections can you make between Paddy O'Toole and Li Chen in "Working on the Transcontinental Railroad, 1869"?

THEME **2** A Place for Us

1. What can you tell about many of the foods we eat based on page 46 of "The World on Your Plate"?

2. In the story "Family Treasures," Hana Koo's family is getting ready to move to Hawaii. How is this information important to the passage?

So Many Kinds of Animals

1. In the story "Slimy, Spiny Riddles," why did Uncle Isaac probably ask so many riddles?

2. Based on the article "Animals," explain how you can infer that there is more than one type of kingdom.

. . . .

THEME 4 Seeds, Fruits, and Flowers

1. How would you describe the sundew from "Mrs. McClary's Very Weird Garden"?

2. If you were to tell a friend about the giant redwood trees in the poem "Ode to the Giant Redwood," how would you describe them?

THEME 5 One Country, Many Regions

1. How can you figure out the meaning of the word <u>currency</u> on page 142 of the story "Who Believes in Buried Treasure?"

2. Explain how clues from the text help you figure out what the word <u>virtual</u> means in the article "Take a Virtual Trip."

THEME 6 The Land Shapes People's Lives

1. What can you tell about Bertie based on page 182 of the story "Mountain Homestead"?

2. What do you learn about the speaker in the last paragraph of "My A-Mazing Summer Vacation"?

THEME 7 Why Does Water Move?

1. Explain why Marguerite and Roberto are on the boat in the story "Typhoon!"

2. Using information from "Fighting Coastal Erosion," explain why it is important to save the wetlands.

....

THEME 8 What Makes Soil Different?

1. Based on information from "The Case of Vanishing Soil," what can people do to safely prevent soil damage?

2. In the story "The Black Blizzard," why does Sam think the Black Blizzard might return?

THEME 9   Native People of North America

1. What connections can you make between the Native Americans in "How the Crow Got Its Color—A Traditional Lakota Tale" and "It's Only Natural"?

2. Using information from the biography "Sequoyah," explain how Sequoyah's work has helped people.

THEME 10   Explorers Arrive

1. Using information from "Jessie Oonark: Inuit Artist," explain how Jessie Oonark decided to become an artist.

2. According to the play "The Return of Ponce de León," why did Ponce de León sail to Florida in the early 1500s?

Life in a Rain Forest

1. Read the "What are you working on now?" section on page 346 of "Meet Janalee P. Caldwell, Frog Detective." Explain whether the information in this section is fact or opinion.

2. Read the first sentence in the story "Walking on the Tree Tops" and explain why the sentence is a fact or an opinion.

....

THEME **12** Affecting the Rain Forest

1. Read "The Balance is Still Broken" on page 364 of "The People of the Rain Forest." Using information from this section, describe how parts of the rain forest probably look.

2. Read the poem "Gorillas in the Wild." Based on details from the poem, how do you imagine gorillas spend their day?

THEME 13   Products and Profits

1. Using information from "A Family Affair," explain what the title of the memoir means.

2. Using information from the play "The Shoemaker's Surprise," explain who the elves helping Henry are.

. . . .

THEME 14   Buying Smart

1. In the poem "Sunday at the Farmers' Market," how are the different sellers at the farmers' market alike?

2. Explain what the four suggestions on page 428 of "Buy! Buy! Why?" have in common.

THEME 15   Earth Long Ago

1. Read the newspaper article "T. Rex Sue Sold to Field Museum." How does knowing the genre help your understanding?

2. How do you know that pages 469 to 472 of "Nate Murphy and the Mystery Sauropod" are part of a journal?

. . . .

THEME 16   Wearing Away

1. Based on information in "Race Against Time: David Sucec Records Ancient Art," why do you think the early artists made their paintings?

2. Read the section, "September 16, 1935," on page 483 of the diary "Saving Mammoth Cave." How would knowing more about what the trees do help you better understand the passage?

Ongoing Test Practice Answer Key

Theme	S	1	2	3	4	5	6
1	D	D	B	C	B	C	Both groups took a risk and moved to California hoping to improve their lives.
2	D	A	B	B	D	A	The main theme of the story is integrating traditions from different cultures.
3	D	B	D	B	C	A	The Italian immigrants wanted to be around people who shared their culture and experiences.
4	D	A	D	B	B	C	The Oak Tree Game Farm is a place you can visit and see animals from all over the world. The animals are often unusual and come from places with neutral climates.
5	B	B	C	A	A	D	A tradition is a way of doing things handed down from one generation to another.
6	D	C	B	D	A	D	The narrator enjoyed the drive-in and will likely go back.
7	B	C	B	A	D	C	Mark Twain based the story of Huck Finn on his own experiences sailing on the Mississippi River as a boy.
8	A	C	D	B	A	B	Picturing a whirlpool as it's described in the story helps you imagine what the base of Niagara Falls is like.
9	C	D	B	C	B	A	People have realized that tomatoes are safe to eat and are delicious. They no longer use them just to decorate; tomatoes are now a common food.
10	C	A	B	C	D	A	Clues: The stones were attached to sticks to make arrows; there is a notch on the arrowhead where it was stuck to the shaft; the arrowhead found was broken, so it may have hit something hard.
11	B	B	A	A	D	C	The last cannot be proved. It is the writer's belief, which other people may disagree with.
12	C	C	D	B	A	D	Details in the passage suggest that Lester grows more relaxed and happy.
13	A	D	A	C	B	D	Archaeologists are a type of scientist. They study Native American history and search for objects from human history.
14	B	D	A	C	C	B	Grandma's orange juice is made from many fruits. Students may also state that Grandma's orange juice is made with love.
15	C	D	A	C	B	C	A newspaper article talks about current events. The event in this passage is a celebration of the 157th birthday of the safety pin.
16	B	B	D	D	A	C	Dr. Koval is probably a paleontologist. He most likely works for a museum or company interested in discovering and preserving fossils.

Extended Response Answer Key

Theme	Question 1	Question 2
1	They lived in the same house and are or came from immigrant families. Both are interested in exploring the past and recording family history.	Both are immigrant workers who escaped poverty and hunger in their homelands to seek their fortunes in America. Both built tracks for the railroad.
2	The foods we eat in the United States have long histories in countries and cultures around the world.	As Hana's family prepares to move, they are reminded of the many family treasures they have and think of ways to preserve these treasures for future generations to enjoy.
3	Uncle Isaac uses riddles to make the information more interesting, to entertain the children, and/or because he is a little strange.	Not every species fits into the animal kingdom. Students may reference the plant kingdom, etc.

Extended Response Answer Key (continued)

Theme	Question 1	Question 2
4	Descriptions should mention that the leaves have sticky little hairs, and students should elaborate on details from the passage.	Descriptions should indicate that the trees are very large and sturdy and have towering limbs that stretch across the sky.
5	Students can figure out the meaning of the word <u>currency</u> by reading the words just before it and the words in the next paragraph.	The descriptive language and illustrations cue the meaning of the word <u>virtual</u> by helping students gain a sense of each place described without actually being there.
6	Details in the text suggest that Bertie is sick.	The speaker is now interested and excited about his trip back to Iowa.
7	Marguerite and Roberto are visiting their Aunt Pilar, who is a biologist.	The wetlands help keep oceans clean, are the homes of animals, and help prevent the erosion of the coastline.
8	People can use natural fertilizer called compost.	Sam thinks the Black Blizzard might return because the blizzards have happened more than once in the past. Also, Sam sees a dark cloud like the one his great-grandfather described.
Mid-Year Review	There are other attractions, air conditioning is available in more places, and travel is easier.	They worked hard, had fun cleaning up the neighborhood, and now want to keep it clean.
9	The native people described in both passages used natural resources to build things they needed to survive.	Sequoyah enabled the Cherokee to communicate in writing and record their history.
10	Jessie was supporting her family and needed the money. She got the idea to become an artist when she saw the kids in school drawing.	Ponce de León had orders from the king of Spain to make a colony in Florida. He also wanted to find the Fountain of Youth.
11	The excerpt is factual because the information can be proved true.	The statement describes personal feelings and cannot be proved true.
12	Descriptions should indicate that parts of the rain forest are being destroyed by construction.	Students should use details from the poem and their imaginations to describe how gorillas spend their day.
13	The title acknowledges the many people who have helped make the speaker's café a success. For the speaker, "family" includes not only his mom, brothers, and sisters, but also his friends, customers, and neighborhood residents.	The handwriting on the note Henry receives from the girls at the end of the play matches the handwriting on the note he receives from the elves earlier in the play.
14	They are all selling things that are either freshly grown or made from freshly grown items.	The four suggestions are all ways that kids can take action against advertising they disagree with.
15	Students know that newspaper articles give facts about a subject and answer the questions *who, what, where, when, why*. They can use their knowledge of newspaper articles to determine the main idea and important points of the article.	These pages are part of a journal because the writer recorded events as he remembered them each day.
16	David Sucec describes the artists as advanced humans. The artists probably used their art to communicate and record their culture and history.	Knowing more about how trees function will help explain how they stop erosion and why the men must plant trees at the cave's entrance.
End-of-Year Review	Pencils are now mostly made of wood, have erasers attached, are painted or varnished, and are available in different styles.	British soldiers were planning to arrest patriots because patriots wanted to be free and spoke out against the king of England.

Name _____

Date _____

Theme Progress Test _____

Name _____

Date _____

Theme Progress Test _____

1 Ⓐ Ⓑ Ⓒ Ⓓ
2 Ⓐ Ⓑ Ⓒ Ⓓ
3 Ⓐ Ⓑ Ⓒ Ⓓ
4 Ⓐ Ⓑ Ⓒ Ⓓ
5 Ⓐ Ⓑ Ⓒ Ⓓ
6 Ⓐ Ⓑ Ⓒ Ⓓ
7 Ⓐ Ⓑ Ⓒ Ⓓ
8 Ⓐ Ⓑ Ⓒ Ⓓ
9 Ⓐ Ⓑ Ⓒ Ⓓ
10 Ⓐ Ⓑ Ⓒ Ⓓ
11 Ⓐ Ⓑ Ⓒ Ⓓ
12 Ⓐ Ⓑ Ⓒ Ⓓ
13 Ⓐ Ⓑ Ⓒ Ⓓ
14 Ⓐ Ⓑ Ⓒ Ⓓ
15 Ⓐ Ⓑ Ⓒ Ⓓ
16 Ⓐ Ⓑ Ⓒ Ⓓ
17 Ⓐ Ⓑ Ⓒ Ⓓ
18 Ⓐ Ⓑ Ⓒ Ⓓ
19 Ⓐ Ⓑ Ⓒ Ⓓ
20 Ⓐ Ⓑ Ⓒ Ⓓ
21 Ⓐ Ⓑ Ⓒ Ⓓ
22 Ⓐ Ⓑ Ⓒ Ⓓ
23 Ⓐ Ⓑ Ⓒ Ⓓ
24 Ⓐ Ⓑ Ⓒ Ⓓ
25 Ⓐ Ⓑ Ⓒ Ⓓ

Name _____

Date _____

Name _____

Date _____

Mid-Year Review

1 Ⓐ Ⓑ Ⓒ Ⓓ	26 Ⓐ Ⓑ Ⓒ Ⓓ
2 Ⓐ Ⓑ Ⓒ Ⓓ	27 Ⓐ Ⓑ Ⓒ Ⓓ
3 Ⓐ Ⓑ Ⓒ Ⓓ	28 Ⓐ Ⓑ Ⓒ Ⓓ
4 Ⓐ Ⓑ Ⓒ Ⓓ	29 Ⓐ Ⓑ Ⓒ Ⓓ
5 Ⓐ Ⓑ Ⓒ Ⓓ	30 Ⓐ Ⓑ Ⓒ Ⓓ
6 Ⓐ Ⓑ Ⓒ Ⓓ	
7 Ⓐ Ⓑ Ⓒ Ⓓ	
8 Ⓐ Ⓑ Ⓒ Ⓓ	
9 Ⓐ Ⓑ Ⓒ Ⓓ	
10 Ⓐ Ⓑ Ⓒ Ⓓ	
11 Ⓐ Ⓑ Ⓒ Ⓓ	
12 Ⓐ Ⓑ Ⓒ Ⓓ	
13 Ⓐ Ⓑ Ⓒ Ⓓ	
14 Ⓐ Ⓑ Ⓒ Ⓓ	
15 Ⓐ Ⓑ Ⓒ Ⓓ	
16 Ⓐ Ⓑ Ⓒ Ⓓ	
17 Ⓐ Ⓑ Ⓒ Ⓓ	
18 Ⓐ Ⓑ Ⓒ Ⓓ	
19 Ⓐ Ⓑ Ⓒ Ⓓ	
20 Ⓐ Ⓑ Ⓒ Ⓓ	
21 Ⓐ Ⓑ Ⓒ Ⓓ	
22 Ⓐ Ⓑ Ⓒ Ⓓ	
23 Ⓐ Ⓑ Ⓒ Ⓓ	
24 Ⓐ Ⓑ Ⓒ Ⓓ	
25 Ⓐ Ⓑ Ⓒ Ⓓ	

End-of-Year Review

1 Ⓐ Ⓑ Ⓒ Ⓓ	26 Ⓐ Ⓑ Ⓒ Ⓓ
2 Ⓐ Ⓑ Ⓒ Ⓓ	27 Ⓐ Ⓑ Ⓒ Ⓓ
3 Ⓐ Ⓑ Ⓒ Ⓓ	28 Ⓐ Ⓑ Ⓒ Ⓓ
4 Ⓐ Ⓑ Ⓒ Ⓓ	29 Ⓐ Ⓑ Ⓒ Ⓓ
5 Ⓐ Ⓑ Ⓒ Ⓓ	30 Ⓐ Ⓑ Ⓒ Ⓓ
6 Ⓐ Ⓑ Ⓒ Ⓓ	31 Ⓐ Ⓑ Ⓒ Ⓓ
7 Ⓐ Ⓑ Ⓒ Ⓓ	32 Ⓐ Ⓑ Ⓒ Ⓓ
8 Ⓐ Ⓑ Ⓒ Ⓓ	33 Ⓐ Ⓑ Ⓒ Ⓓ
9 Ⓐ Ⓑ Ⓒ Ⓓ	34 Ⓐ Ⓑ Ⓒ Ⓓ
10 Ⓐ Ⓑ Ⓒ Ⓓ	35 Ⓐ Ⓑ Ⓒ Ⓓ
11 Ⓐ Ⓑ Ⓒ Ⓓ	36 Ⓐ Ⓑ Ⓒ Ⓓ
12 Ⓐ Ⓑ Ⓒ Ⓓ	37 Ⓐ Ⓑ Ⓒ Ⓓ
13 Ⓐ Ⓑ Ⓒ Ⓓ	38 Ⓐ Ⓑ Ⓒ Ⓓ
14 Ⓐ Ⓑ Ⓒ Ⓓ	39 Ⓐ Ⓑ Ⓒ Ⓓ
15 Ⓐ Ⓑ Ⓒ Ⓓ	40 Ⓐ Ⓑ Ⓒ Ⓓ
16 Ⓐ Ⓑ Ⓒ Ⓓ	41 Ⓐ Ⓑ Ⓒ Ⓓ
17 Ⓐ Ⓑ Ⓒ Ⓓ	42 Ⓐ Ⓑ Ⓒ Ⓓ
18 Ⓐ Ⓑ Ⓒ Ⓓ	43 Ⓐ Ⓑ Ⓒ Ⓓ
19 Ⓐ Ⓑ Ⓒ Ⓓ	44 Ⓐ Ⓑ Ⓒ Ⓓ
20 Ⓐ Ⓑ Ⓒ Ⓓ	45 Ⓐ Ⓑ Ⓒ Ⓓ
21 Ⓐ Ⓑ Ⓒ Ⓓ	46 Ⓐ Ⓑ Ⓒ Ⓓ
22 Ⓐ Ⓑ Ⓒ Ⓓ	47 Ⓐ Ⓑ Ⓒ Ⓓ
23 Ⓐ Ⓑ Ⓒ Ⓓ	48 Ⓐ Ⓑ Ⓒ Ⓓ
24 Ⓐ Ⓑ Ⓒ Ⓓ	49 Ⓐ Ⓑ Ⓒ Ⓓ
25 Ⓐ Ⓑ Ⓒ Ⓓ	50 Ⓐ Ⓑ Ⓒ Ⓓ

Writing Checklist

Read the writing prompt. Use the prompt to write a well-organized paper. Use the checklist below to help you improve your writing.

☐ I read the prompt carefully.

☐ I used prewriting strategies to organize my ideas.

☐ I used neat and clear handwriting.

☐ I expressed my ideas clearly.

☐ I organized my ideas clearly.

☐ I supported my ideas with details and examples.

☐ I wrote a clear beginning, middle, and end.

☐ I used interesting words that mean exactly what I want to say.

☐ I wrote different types of sentences.

☐ I made sure my writing sounds right and makes sense.

☐ I revised confusing parts of my writing to make them clearer.

☐ I proofread my writing.

☐ I edited for capital letters.

☐ I edited for correct punctuation.

☐ I edited for correct spelling.

☐ I took out unnecessary words and details.

Make sure you have looked at every item in the checklist to make your writing better.

Name _____ Date _____